1,000 FACTS ABOUT ANCIENT EGYPT

NANCY HONOVICH   FOREWORD BY DR. JENNIFER HOUSER WEGNER

NATIONAL GEOGRAPHIC

WASHINGTON, D.C.

TABLE OF CONTENTS

Great Temple of Ramses II at Abu Simbel, Egypt

Ancient Egypt is fascinating and mysterious. The civilization that thrived along the Nile River thousands of years ago continues to captivate us today. This book introduces you to all of the wonders of ancient Egypt.

The land of Egypt is mostly desert, but through the middle of this hot, dry environment, the life-giving Nile River flows from south to north. Along its banks, the Egyptians created one of the world's most impressive ancient civilizations—a land governed by powerful rulers and watched over by many gods and goddesses.

These rulers varied from mighty warriors, for example Thutmose III and Ramses II, to the famous Tutankhamun, who was only a child when he came to power. In a land where the pharaoh was supposed to be a man, a few exceptional women—such as Hatshepsut and Cleopatra—occupied the throne. Ancient Egyptians believed these rulers worked hand in hand with the gods to protect Egypt and its people.

But ancient Egypt wasn't just about royalty and the divine. Thanks to the work of scholars and researchers, we know a great deal about the daily life of nonroyal people from all walks of life, from the wealthy official to the peasant farmer. We know where they lived, what they ate, and how they dressed. We can visualize the jobs they had and how they spent their free time.

The Egyptians believed in a life after death. Because of this they worked hard to mummify their dead and to provide a good burial. The Egyptians built soaring pyramids and hidden tombs to protect the body of the deceased and their grave goods as they made the passage to the afterlife. Artists and craftsmen created dazzling works of art, such as statues, jewelry, and vessels of pottery and stone. These objects, along with things like clothing and furniture, were buried with the deceased, for it was believed they would be needed in the afterlife.

Along with many innovations in architecture, science, medicine, and mathematics, the Egyptians developed a complex writing system comprised of hundreds of hieroglyphic signs that remained in use for more than 3,000 years. Thanks to the work of Jean-François Champollion—who was the first to decipher Egyptian hieroglyphs—and countless other scholars who came after him, we can read the inscriptions the Egyptians left behind carved in stone or written on papyrus. Through these writings we can learn more about the world of the ancient Egyptians.

When I am asked why I became an Egyptologist, I tell people that my sixth grade social studies teacher introduced me to the wonders of the ancient world. I was captivated by stories of discoveries made by archaeologists like Howard Carter, who discovered the tomb of Tutankhamun in 1922, and I was intrigued by the idea of cracking the code of Egyptian hieroglyphs. Ancient Egypt seemed like a puzzle that needed to be solved.

Important discoveries continue to be made in the field of Egyptology. Exploration of Egypt continues today, with active archaeological projects throughout the country uncovering temples, tombs, and town sites and making exciting finds. More and more, Egyptologists are using all sorts of new technologies to aid in their work. We know so much about ancient Egypt, but there is still so much more to learn. The sands of Egypt still have many hidden stories to tell!

Dr. Jennifer Houser Wegner
Department of Near Eastern Languages and Civilizations
University of Pennsylvania, U.S.A.

FACTS, DATES, AND RULERS' NAMES

Inside this book, you'll find 1,000 facts about the people, culture, society, religion, and everyday life of ancient Egypt. At the back, you'll find a glossary, which has definitions of special words and terms used in the book. There is also a timeline of key events in the history of ancient Egypt—and a list of dynasties and rulers. Note that dates given in this book are estimates based on historical data, which in some periods are poor or missing. Also, the names of rulers have been translated from an ancient language and vary among scholars, so you may find different spellings for these in other reference books.

10 FAST FACTS ABOUT

1
MORE THAN **90 PERCENT** OF EGYPT IS COVERED IN **HOT DESERT.**

2
Many ancient Egyptians were descendants of hunters and fishermen who settled near the Nile River nearly 8,000 years ago.

3
The soil along the banks of the Nile was suitable for FARMING, so the early settlers began to grow CROPS such as GRAIN.

4
THE **COMMUNITIES THAT LIVED** AROUND THE NILE WERE **UNITED AS A KINGDOM** IN 3100 B.C.

5
AT THE **HEIGHT OF ITS POWER,** FROM 1504 TO 1450 B.C. ANCIENT EGYPT SPANNED FROM THE **NILE VALLEY** TO PARTS OF PRESENT-DAY **SYRIA, ISRAEL,** AND **JORDAN.**

6
Ancient Egyptians sometimes called their homeland KEMET, meaning "BLACK LAND." The term refers to the DARK MUD from the Nile.

ANCIENT EGYPT

7 For about 500 years Egyptians built PYRAMIDS, which they used as ROYAL TOMBS. Many of these pyramids still stand today.

8 Ancient Egyptians spoke a LANGUAGE that has similarities to ARABIC, HEBREW, and some AFRICAN TRIBAL languages.

9 Over almost 3,000 years 30 DIFFERENT DYNASTIES—or families—RULED ancient Egypt.

10 AFTER ABOUT 1000 B.C. ANCIENT EGYPT'S POWER BEGAN TO WEAKEN AS THE KINGDOM LOST SOME OF ITS WEALTH AND LAND AND BROKE UP INTO SMALLER PARTS.

Pyramids at Giza

THE LAND OF ANCIENT EGYPT

Two Regions: Upper Egypt and Lower Egypt

Before ancient Egypt was united as a single kingdom, it was divided into two main regions—Upper Egypt and Lower Egypt. Since the Nile River flows from south to north, the southern region was called Upper Egypt and the northern region was called Lower Egypt.

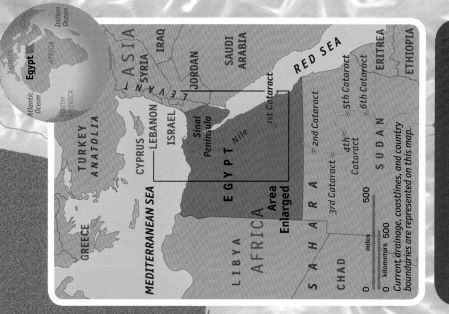

Current drainage, coastlines, and country boundaries are represented on this map.

LINKING CONTINENTS

The land of ancient Egypt was a narrow strip along the northern section of the Nile River, which starts in the heartland of Africa. The Sinai Peninsula is a bridge between Africa and Asia.

Memphis

Memphis was the capital city during the early years of the unified kingdom of ancient Egypt. It was located just south of the Nile Delta. Several pharaohs built pyramids, such as the Great Pyramids at Giza, just outside Memphis.

Nile Delta

The Nile flows from highlands south of Egypt. Before it empties into the Mediterranean Sea, the river splits into branches that fan out in a triangular shape. This area, known as the Nile Delta, encompassed Lower Egypt and is one of the world's most fertile farming areas.

SAUDI
ARABIA

S i n a i

RED SEA

WESTERN
DESERT

Red Sea Hills

MAP KEY

▬ Fertile land
☐ Ancient Egyptian site
= Cataract
• Modern city

| 0 | miles | 50 |
| 0 | kilometers | 50 |

Current drainage, coastlines, and country boundaries are represented on this map.

Desert

The Nile Valley is surrounded by two deserts— the Western and the Eastern. In ancient times, these rocky, sandy regions protected Egypt from invaders. The Egyptians called the desert *desheret,* which means "red land."

Nile Valley Cliffs

Limestone and sandstone cliffs near the river's edge provided ancient Egyptians with materials to build structures such as pyramids and temples.

Mountains

A small mountain range, sometimes called the Red Sea Hills, runs from north to south in the Eastern Desert. Here ancient Egyptians mined precious stones and minerals, such as gold.

E A S T E R N   D E S E R T

U P P E R

E G Y P T

Beni Hasan

Hermopolis

Amarna
(Akhetaten)

Cusae
(Kusai)

Asyut

This
(Tjeny)

Abydos
(Abedju)

Dendera
(Dandara)

Naqada
(Nubt)

Valley of
the Kings

Luxor
(Thebes, Waset)

Nile

Esna
(Isna)

Nekhen
(Hierakonpolis)

Edfu
(Idfu)

Aswan
(Syene)

Elephantine Island
1st Cataract
Philae
Aswân High Dam

Kalabsha
(Talmis)

N U B I A

*Lake
Nasser*

Thebes

Around 2040 B.C. Thebes became ancient Egypt's capital. The city, located in Upper Egypt, was home to many famous monuments, including Karnak Temple and Luxor Temple, as well as towering structures known as obelisks. Today, eastern Thebes is called Luxor.

11

1 The ANCIENT EGYPTIAN CIVILIZATION lasted for almost 3,000 YEARS, ending around 30 B.C.

2 During the height of ANCIENT EGYPT'S power, its POPULATION may have reached THREE MILLION.

3 MORE THAN 96 MILLION PEOPLE LIVE IN EGYPT TODAY.

4 THE AVERAGE ANCIENT EGYPTIAN WOMAN LIVED TO BE ABOUT 30 YEARS OLD, WHILE THE AVERAGE MAN LIVED TO BE ABOUT 34 YEARS OLD.

5 Historians believe RAMSES II, a famous ancient Egyptian ruler, LIVED BEYOND the AGE of 80.

25 NUMBER-CRUNCHING FACTS

6 RAMSES II had more than 100 CHILDREN. At least 52 were sons.

7 Instead of letters and words, ancient Egyptians used more than 6,000 SYMBOLS called HIEROGLYPHS to write texts.

8 Ancient Egyptians used the same hieroglyph for ZERO as they did for BEAUTY.

9 THE EGYPTIAN SYMBOL FOR ONE MILLION WAS A GOD WITH HIS ARMS RAISED WIDE.

12 In 1954, scientists discovered a 4,600-year-old BOAT that belonged to the ancient Egyptian ruler KHUFU.

10 THERE WERE ONLY THREE WEEKS IN AN ANCIENT EGYPTIAN MONTH.

11 BOYS who received a formal education in ancient Egypt STARTED SCHOOL when they were about FIVE YEARS OLD. Few girls had a formal education.

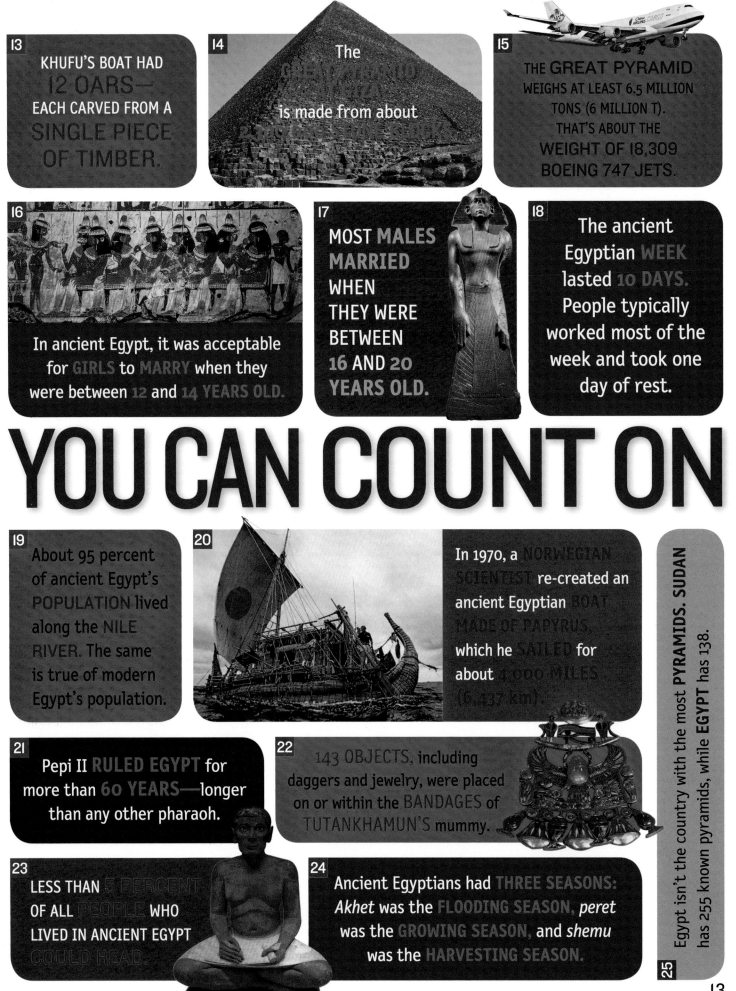

13
KHUFU'S BOAT HAD **12 OARS**— EACH CARVED FROM A **SINGLE PIECE OF TIMBER.**

14
The **GREAT PYRAMID OF GIZA** is made from about **2.3 MILLION STONE BLOCKS.**

15
THE **GREAT PYRAMID** WEIGHS AT LEAST 6.5 MILLION TONS (6 MILLION T). THAT'S ABOUT THE WEIGHT OF 18,309 BOEING 747 JETS.

16
In ancient Egypt, it was acceptable for **GIRLS** to **MARRY** when they were between **12** and **14 YEARS OLD.**

17
MOST MALES MARRIED WHEN THEY WERE BETWEEN 16 AND 20 YEARS OLD.

18
The ancient Egyptian **WEEK** lasted **10 DAYS.** People typically worked most of the week and took one day of rest.

YOU CAN COUNT ON

19
About 95 percent of ancient Egypt's **POPULATION** lived along the **NILE RIVER.** The same is true of modern Egypt's population.

20
In 1970, a **NORWEGIAN SCIENTIST** re-created an ancient Egyptian **BOAT MADE OF PAPYRUS,** which he **SAILED** for about 4,000 MILES (6,437 km).

21
Pepi II **RULED EGYPT** for more than **60 YEARS**—longer than any other pharaoh.

22
143 OBJECTS, including daggers and jewelry, were placed on or within the BANDAGES of TUTANKHAMUN'S mummy.

23
LESS THAN 5 PERCENT OF ALL PEOPLE WHO LIVED IN ANCIENT EGYPT COULD READ.

24
Ancient Egyptians had **THREE SEASONS:** *Akhet* was the **FLOODING SEASON,** *peret* was the **GROWING SEASON,** and *shemu* was the **HARVESTING SEASON.**

25
Egypt isn't the country with the most **PYRAMIDS. SUDAN** has 255 known pyramids, while **EGYPT** has 138.

1
Ancient Egyptians worshipped approximately 2,000 gods and goddesses.

2
Most Egyptians believed that all gods stemmed from one creator god, but the name and nature of that god varied between regions.

3
Ptah is one of the oldest Egyptian creator gods. He was originally worshipped in Memphis, but later had followers throughout Egypt.

4
According to one myth, Ptah simply uttered the names of living creatures to create them.

5
People who lived on Elephantine Island worshipped Khnum as the creator god.

6
Ra was a creator god who was believed to have formed humans from his tears.

7
The Egyptians associated Ra with the sun and believed that each day he died at sunset and was reborn at sunrise.

8
Ra created Shu, the god of air and wind.

9
Tefnut, the goddess of moisture, was Ra's daughter. Tefnut had a lioness's head.

10
Geb was the god of the Earth. Ancient Egyptians believed his laughter caused earthquakes.

11
Anubis, the god of mummification, is depicted with the head of a jackal because Egyptians often saw these animals around cemeteries.

12
The Egyptians believed that Tayet, the goddess of weaving, crafted the bandages used to wrap mummies.

13
They also believed that Hapi, the god of the Nile, lived in a cave beneath Elephantine Island in the Nile River.

14
Thoth was a moon god who invented writing. He kept records of the dead.

15
Isis—a mother goddess known for her magic power—mourned the dead with her sister Nephthys, a funerary goddess.

16
Isis was married to Osiris, a god who ruled the underworld and once lived on Earth in human form.

17
According to one legend, Osiris was murdered by his brother, Seth, but was reborn after Isis mummified him.

18
Ancient Egyptians believed that Osiris was the first ever mummy.

19
Sobek was a crocodile god who loved to eat flesh, especially the flesh of Egypt's enemies.

20
Ancient Egyptians believed that crocodiles had no tongues because Sobek had his removed. In reality, crocodiles have stunted tongues.

21
Wadjet was a cobra goddess who, along with Nekhbet, a vulture goddess, protected Egypt's king.

22
Bastet was a cat goddess who was associated with music and dance. She was often shown holding a sistrum, an instrument that rattles when shaken.

23
As a result of her association with cats, which have a nurturing instinct, Bastet became the protector of pregnant women.

24
Hathor, a cow goddess, was associated with the Milky Way. The Egyptians believed the Milky Way was the milk that flowed from her udders.

25
Hathor loved stones and metals, and she became the patron goddess of miners.

26
Sekhmet was a lioness-headed goddess and the daughter of Ra.

27
Ancient Egyptians believed that hot desert winds and plagues were produced by Sekhmet.

28
Seth was the god of chaos, storms, and deserts. He is often depicted as a donkey, pig, or hippopotamus.

29
Horus, the falcon-headed god, lost his eye in a battle against Seth—but the eye was magically restored.

30
The Eye of Horus was a symbol inspired by this myth. It represented health, healing, and protection.

31
Bes was a patron god of childbirth and the home. His image was often carved into furniture and other household items.

32 Apep, the spirit of darkness and destruction—is often depicted as a coiled snake.

33 To ward off evil associated with Apep, some ancient Egyptian priests destroyed a model of a snake.

36 Some scholars believe that Amentet, the Egyptian goddess of the west, originated in what is now Libya.

39 After an Apis bull died, the Egyptians would mummify the animal's corpse.

45 Sirius, a star that appears near the Orion constellation, was believed to be Sodpet, a goddess married to Sahu.

34 The goddess Taweret, who protected pregnant women and children, was the female counterpart to Bes.

37 Ancient Egyptians associated the sun setting in the west with death, so Amentet also became a funerary goddess.

40 Nefertum was born from a blue lotus flower bud and thus became the god of perfume.

46 Sodpet's star appeared in the night sky just before the flood season. So the Egyptians considered Sodpet an agricultural goddess.

35 Taweret had the head of a hippopotamus, the tail of a crocodile, and the paws of a lion.

38 If a bull was born with certain black and white markings, it was believed to be a living form of the fertility god, Apis.

41 Various scorpion species lived in the Egyptian deserts and could kill people with their stings. Selket, a scorpion goddess, offered protection from the stings.

47 Heka was the god of magic and was often depicted as a cobra or a cobra-headed human.

42 Seshat, the goddess of writing, kept records of the goods that ancient Egyptian kings seized in battle. These included sheep, cattle, and goats.

48 Anat was a warrior goddess who protected ancient Egypt's ruler during battle.

43 Benu was a mythical bird with the head of a heron and the body of a hawk that was linked to the gods of creation and the sun.

49 It was believed that Shai, the god of destiny, determined the length of a person's life.

44 Ancient Egyptians identified the constellation Orion with their star god, Sahu, who was visible only at night.

50 Satis was a goddess who guarded Egypt's southern region with her arrows.

Egyptian gods from the Temple of Sobek

50
Heavenly Facts About
GODS AND GODDESSES

1 The Nile River, which flows for about 4,160 miles (6,695 km), is the **longest river in Africa.**

2 **In addition to Egypt,** the Nile River **flows through 10 countries:** Burundi, the Democratic Republic of the Congo, Eritrea, Ethiopia, Kenya, Rwanda, Sudan, South Sudan, Tanzania, and Uganda.

3 Most experts agree that the Nile River is **formed by waters** flowing from Lake Victoria and the **Rwenzori Mountains,** both in eastern Africa.

4 The Nile River is home to the **world's largest freshwater fish,** the Nile perch, which can grow up to **six feet (1.8 m) in length.**

5 A **tiny island** called Elephantine sits in the **middle of the Nile.** Elephantine was ancient Egypt's southernmost city.

6 The Egyptians used the Nile as a **highway.** They **steered boats** along the river using oars mounted on the stern.

7 **Sailing upriver** against the current required help from the wind. So they **hoisted large sails** on their boats.

ABOUT THE NILE

8 Papyrus—a reed plant that grows in the river's marshes—was used to make small boats and a paperlike material, also called papyrus.

9 During floods, **dark sediments** flowed through the river, giving it a dark appearance.

10 The Nile flows at a rate of 829,000 gallons a second (3 million L/sec).

11 **Heavy rains** and **melting snow** from southern highlands caused the Nile to flood each year. Today, several **dams** are used to control the flooding.

12 The Egyptians used special wells called **nilometers** to measure the water level of the river during the **flooding**.

13 Ancient Egyptians believed that Hapi, the **god of the Nile**, was responsible for the floods.

14 The population relied on **fish in the river**—including catfish and perch—as a **food source**. They caught the fish with nets, hooks, and spears.

15 The Nile has six major **cataracts**, or areas **where white-water rapids tumble over rocks.** The cataracts were difficult to navigate and **kept enemy ships away.**

Nile River at Aswan

1 Tutankhamun became famous in 1922, when British archaeologist HOWARD CARTER discovered the Egyptian ruler's TOMB.

2 Tutankhamun's tomb was discovered in the VALLEY OF THE KINGS, a burial ground where other pharaohs were also entombed.

3 Rumors of a MUMMY'S CURSE spread after Lord Carnarvon, an amateur Egyptologist involved in Howard Carter's expedition, DIED from a mosquito-borne disease after entering the tomb.

4 Tutankhamun was nicknamed the "BOY KING" because he was only NINE YEARS OLD when he became the ruler of Egypt.

5 King Tutankhamun RULED FOR ONLY 10 YEARS and died at the age of 19.

25 DUG-UP FACTS ABOUT KING

6 A **GOLD BURIAL MASK** was placed over Tutankhamun's head. The face formed on the mask may show what the king looked like.

7 THE BURIAL MASK'S HEADDRESS FEATURES A vulture, REPRESENTING TUTANKHAMUN'S RULE OVER Upper Egypt, AND A cobra, REPRESENTING HIS RULE OVER Lower Egypt.

8 Tutankhamun's MUMMY was placed inside THREE COFFINS. The innermost coffin was made of SOLID GOLD.

9 The mummy and three coffins were sealed inside a large stone structure called a SARCOPHAGUS.

10 THE CAUSE OF THE KING'S death remains a mystery. SOME THEORIES INCLUDE A CHARIOT CRASH, AN ACCIDENT, OR A DISEASE.

11 Tutankhamun believed his spirit would survive death, so he was BURIED WITH 365 STATUES that would act as SERVANTS in the afterlife.

12 The tomb contained WOODEN CHESTS FILLED WITH CLOTHING— including 100 pairs of sandals.

13 SIX CHARIOTS were discovered inside the tomb. Some were large and likely used during ceremonies, while others were small and intended for EVERYDAY use.

14 Tutankhamun's chariots had wheels with TIRES and SPOKES of FLEXIBLE WOOD that absorbed shocks on rough surfaces.

15 Tutankhamun's father declared Aten, a sun god, the most important Egyptian god. Tutankhamun later REPLACED ATEN WITH AMUN, a creator god.

16 Tutankhamun, which means "living image of Amun," is NOT THE KING'S ORIGINAL NAME. He changed it from Tutankhaten, meaning "living image of Aten."

17 TUTANKHAMUN'S TOMB measured only 1,184 square feet (110 sq m). That's about HALF THE SIZE of a TENNIS COURT.

TUTANKHAMUN

18 A SCAN OF TUTANKHAMUN'S BODY SHOWS THAT HE SUFFERED A FRACTURED THIGH BONE SHORTLY BEFORE HE DIED.

19 Scientists have found NO CAVITIES in Tutankhamun's teeth.

20 Tutankhamun GREW UP in a palace located in a city called AMARNA, where he was likely cared for by royal nurses.

21 A DAGGER in the king's tomb was probably made from a METEORITE, a rock that fell from space.

22 A PAINTING on the tomb wall DEPICTS TUTANKHAMUN AS OSIRIS, a god who died and was reborn.

24 DURING CEREMONIES, TUTANKHAMUN LIKELY CARRIED A CROOK, A STICK OFTEN USED BY SHEPHERDS, AND A FLAIL, A TYPE OF WHIP.

23 Tutankhamun's organs—including his LUNGS, LIVER, and INTESTINES—were removed when he died and SEALED in separate CONTAINERS.

25 In 2017, a large STATUE was unearthed along the Nile. Experts believe the statue depicts QUEEN TIYE—Tutankhamun's GRANDMOTHER.

1 Egyptians believed a person's **spirit survived death.** If the body was destroyed, the spirit might be lost, so they **mummified the body** to preserve it.

2 The mummy-making process took about **70 days to complete.**

3 Embalmers were responsible for making mummies. They were supervised by a priest who wore a jackal mask to represent Anubis — the god of mummification.

4 To begin the mummy-making process, the embalmers **inserted a hook** through the dead person's nose and up into the brain. The brain was then **mashed** and pulled out, or it drained out.

5 Sticky tree sap called resin was poured in through the nostrils to plug up the empty brain cavity.

6 The embalmers also made a cut in the left side of the body, from which they **removed four organs—the liver, lungs, intestines,** and **stomach.**

7 Each organ was placed in a jar crafted in the image of a god. Such jars were called "canopic," possibly after Canopus, a city linked with Osiris, god of the dead.

Anubis attends to the mummy of Sennedjem, an important craftworker.

8 The Egyptians believed that **the spirit needed the heart** in the afterlife, so they **kept this organ inside** the body.

9 To help **remove unpleasant odors,** the embalmers washed the body with water and wine.

10 The embalmers **covered the body in a salt called natron** for about 40 days. The salt prevented decay by sucking out the body's moisture.

11 After the embalmers removed the natron, they **stuffed the body** with linen pads, mud, and sawdust **to help keep its shape.**

12 **Resin and beeswax** were often slathered over the dried body to **seal out water** and ward off bacteria, which cause decay.

13 The embalmers spent about **15 days wrapping the body** in linen bandages.

14 The **amount of linen** used to wrap a single mummy could cover **three-quarters of a professional basketball court.**

15 A **mask with the person's facial features** was placed over the mummy's face so that, in the afterlife, a spirit could identify its body.

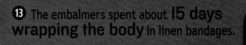

15 POINTED FACTS ABOUT

① **Before pyramids** were built, the Egyptians buried their dead rulers beneath flat-roof **structures called mastabas.**

② The Step Pyramid, built as a tomb for King Djoser more than 4,600 years ago, is the **oldest known pyramid in Egypt.**

③ The **Step Pyramid** started as a **mastaba,** but Djoser wanted something grander so, before his death, he had **five layers added** to the top.

④ King Snefru was determined to make a **pyramid with smooth sides,** but his first effort resulted in the **awkward-looking Bent Pyramid.** No mummies were buried there.

⑤ Snefru then built the **smooth-sided North, or "Red," Pyramid,** nicknamed for the reddish color of its stones. Snefru's burial place is unknown.

⑥ The **Great Pyramid at Giza is Egypt's largest pyramid.** It stands 481 feet (147 m) tall. That's taller than 33 double-decker buses stacked.

⑦ Most of the **workers** hired to **construct the Great Pyramid** as a tomb for King Khufu around 2530 B.C. were **farmers** and not skilled masons.

THE PYRAMIDS

Pyramid of Khafre and the Great Sphinx at Giza

8 Some pyramid tops, or **capstones,** were made from **granite,** a hard stone that had to be hammered out with tools called **dolerite pounders.**

9 The stone blocks used to build the Great Pyramid each weighed about 2.5 tons (2.3 t). That's about the weight of 20 baby elephants.

10 The core of many pyramids was made from **blocks of limestone,** a soft rock that could be cut using copper chisels.

11 To move heavy stones from the quarry, workers placed them on ramps dampened with water, and then had teams of oxen pull them.

12 At the pyramid construction site, Egyptian men likely hauled the stones by **pulling them on wooden logs.**

13 Inside the Great Pyramid, a long, narrow passageway called the Grand Gallery leads to two chambers known as the **Queen's Chamber** and the **King's Chamber.**

14 Khufu's body was originally placed inside a sarcophagus in the **King's Chamber,** but it was later stolen by tomb robbers.

15 The purpose of the Queen's Chamber remains a mystery. Khufu is believed to have had **three wives,** but **none were buried inside the pyramid.**

1 In ANCIENT EGYPT, most clothing was made from LINEN, a lightweight fabric.

2 Linen was made from the FIBERS OF THE FLAX PLANT, which was grown on the estates of wealthy Egyptians.

3 Young CHILDREN wore no clothing, but they did wear jewelry such as EARRINGS and BRACELETS.

4 AROUND 1000 B.C. A LONG, DRESSLIKE GARMENT BECAME FASHIONABLE FOR MEN AND WOMEN.

5 Some DRESSES were FITTED, others loose. They were SLEEVED or SLEEVELESS and with or without SHOULDER STRAPS.

25 FASHION-FORWARD FACTS ABOUT

6 A *SHENDYT* is a skirt shown in many Egyptian artworks. It was probably worn by men while RUNNING, HUNTING, or during COMBAT.

7 Most CLOTHING was WHITE, which kept the Egyptians cool. However, the royal family occasionally wore colored clothes made with PLANT-DYED FABRICS.

8 Royal clothing was sometimes EMBROIDERED with yarn that was twisted with STRANDS OF GOLD.

9 KINGS and PRIESTS wore ANIMAL SKINS fastened around their shoulders. They believed the animal TRANSFERRED ITS POWERS to the wearer.

10 RULERS of ancient Egypt were known to wear skirts decorated with a BULL'S TAIL.

11 Wealthy people wore SANDALS made from pieces of either LEATHER or PLANTS woven together and then decorated.

12 Upper-class women wore LONG SHAWLS that resembled saris, which were draped over the shoulder, wrapped around the body, and tied to the waist by a cord.

13 On CHILLY EVENINGS, Egyptians wore as outer garments WOOL CLOAKS that were made from the hair of goats or sheep.

14 The KING'S SANDALS were often gold and decorated with pictures of EGYPT'S ENEMIES so that he could symbolically CRUSH them as he walked.

17 Women sometimes wore BEADED, NETLIKE DRESSES over fitted garments.

15 KINGS USUALLY WORE A RED CROWN WHEN RULING LOWER EGYPT AND A WHITE CROWN WHEN RULING UPPER EGYPT. THE CROWNS WERE SOMETIMES JOINED AS A SYMBOL OF A UNIFIED EGYPT.

16 The *hemhemet* crown, which featured THREE SEPARATE CROWNS mounted on a pair of RAM'S HORNS, was worn by rulers during ceremonies.

18 Men and women wore PLEATED GARMENTS that were stiffened to give them shape.

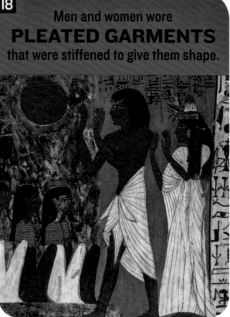

STYLE

19 Paintings of King Ramses III show him WEARING A SASH wrapped several times around his torso like a girdle.

20 Ramses III's "girdle" was DECORATED WITH ANKH SYMBOLS. In ancient Egypt "ankh" meant "life," and the symbols were believed to protect the king on the battlefield.

21 MEN'S SKIRTS became LONGER OVER TIME. The skirts were originally knee-length, but later it became fashionable to wear them at ankle-length.

22 Most men and women wore triangular linen LOINCLOTHS as UNDERWEAR.

23 SOLDIERS may have required sturdier undergarments, so their LOINCLOTHS were made from LEATHER.

24 Priests DRESSED STATUES OF GODS in linen garments, headbands, and neck collars.

25 The ancient Egyptian word *mut* was used for both vulture and mother, so QUEENS wore a VULTURE HEADDRESS. It was a sign of their duty to produce a royal heir—the next ruler of Egypt.

15 SACRED FACTS ABOUT

1 Ancient Egyptian religion included stories about gods who controlled the sun, moon, and floods. The Egyptians made up these stories because **they did not understand** how these **natural phenomena** happened.

2 Stone temples were built throughout ancient Egypt to **honor various gods.** They were large buildings with many rooms and columns.

3 Ancient Egyptian priests were servants of gods who looked after the temples.

4 At a new king's **coronation ceremony,** priests poured water on the king to **purify him** and announced his **powers over the people.**

5 Priests had specific jobs. Some tended to statues of gods, some oversaw funerals, while others studied astronomy or measured hours of the day.

6 To **purify himself** for the gods, a **priest shaved his head and body** and **chewed** balls of salt called **natron** to clean his mouth.

7 Priests conducted the Opening of the Mouth ceremony where they acted as if to open a dead person's eyes and mouth to bring the deceased's spirit to life.

RELIGION AND RITUAL

ancient Egyptian gods on a painted wooden stela

8 Priests were **not allowed to wear wool or leather** against their skin because clothing made from animals was not considered pure.

9 Ancient Egyptian religion was based on the idea that truth and justice were needed to maintain *Maat*, or order and harmony in the universe.

10 The Egyptians believed **Maat was present during peaceful times** but missing during times of war and unrest.

11 It was believed that every living person, whatever their class, would be judged in the afterlife by 42 gods.

12 Ancient Egyptians believed that the heart **contained a record of a person's actions,** so they left it inside the mummy for the gods to judge.

13 The gods weighed the heart on a balance scale against a feather. If the balance's beam was level, the heart and feather weighed the same, and the spirit could live on in the afterlife.

14 The Egyptians believed **wrongdoers had heavy hearts.** If the heart outweighed the gods' feather, it was **eaten by a monster** called Ammut, the "Devourer."

15 The Egyptians buried mummies with the **Book of the Dead,** a collection of spells that would **help the deceased make the passage to the afterlife.**

75 EVERYDAY FACTS ABOUT DAILY LIFE

1 Ancient Egyptians showed one another affection by rubbing noses and kissing.

2 Since pigs eat just about anything, they may have been used to clean food waste from the streets of ancient Egyptian settlements.

3 Other garbage was collected by people and sometimes burned outside of town.

4 Royal officials occasionally took a census, or count, of all the people and cattle in Egypt.

5 **MIDDLE-CLASS HOUSES WERE BUILT IN CROWDED AREAS AND COULD BE TWO OR THREE STORIES HIGH.**

6 In multistory houses, ramps or stairs on the outside of the buildings connected the floors.

7 Houses were made of sun-dried mud bricks, which kept houses cool in the summer and warm in the winter.

8 To make the bricks, river mud was mixed with straw, sand, and pebbles and poured into molds.

9 The mud bricks were placed in the sun to bake for several days. Once they hardened they could be used for construction.

10 Wood was expensive, so only wealthier Egyptians had roofs made of timber.

11 Poorer people lived together in cramped conditions, in small huts with roofs made from straw, reeds, or grass.

12 To keep smoke and cooking smells at bay, kitchens were located away from the main living quarters of a house.

13 Cooking was done either in clay ovens or over open fires.

14 Only wealthy children received a formal education.

15 Childless couples were encouraged to adopt so that they could have someone to look after them in old age.

16 Ancient Egyptians kept busts of their ancestors in the home. They believed they could communicate with their dead family members through these busts.

17 Ancient Egyptians sometimes married non-Egyptians. An artifact called the Stela of Nenu depicts a marriage between an Egyptian woman and a Nubian man.

18 Young girls were responsible for helping their mothers with household chores and watching over younger siblings.

19 Boys were expected to follow in their fathers' career. They served as apprentices until they could do the job themselves.

20 **IN ADDITION TO CLOTHING, LINEN WAS USED FOR BEDSHEETS.**

21 Wooden headrests were used as pillows.

22 Some ancient Egyptians had chairs and stools with seats made from basketry.

23 The chairs and couches of wealthy Egyptians were often made from a dark wood called ebony.

24 **EGYPTIAN WOMEN GAVE BIRTH ON BRICKS THAT WERE DECORATED WITH SCENES OF GODS AND CHILDBIRTH.**

25 The Egyptians used birth bricks to call on the gods to protect the mother and newborn child.

26 After marriage, many ancient Egyptian couples lived with the husband's or wife's parents.

27 A letter written by a royal official named Hekanakht notes that at least 18 people lived in his house.

28 Ancient Egyptians often married family members—mostly cousins and rarely brothers or sisters.

29 Wealthy couples often had documents called marriage contracts, which included a list of the couple's possessions.

30 There was no formal marriage ceremony. The bride simply moved into her husband's home with her possessions.

31 **CHILDREN'S SCHOOLS HAD CLASSROOMS WITH BENCHES FOR STUDENTS TO SIT ON AND LESSONS WRITTEN ON WALLS.**

32 Classroom walls also featured rules encouraging students to work hard and master their argument skills.

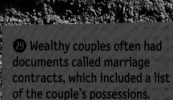

33 Babies and toddlers were fed liquids such as milk from a small cup with a spout.

34 Infant feeding cups were usually decorated with pictures of gods to protect the child from harm.

35 WINDOWS IN HOUSES WERE SET HIGH UP ON WALLS TO KEEP ROOMS COOL IN THE SUMMER AND WARM IN THE WINTER.

36 During warm summer nights, Egyptians sometimes slept outdoors on the flat roof of the house.

37 The walls of wealthy people's homes were decorated on the inside with colorful frescoes.

38 To light their homes, people used oil lamps that consisted of a saucer of oil and a long, floating wick.

39 Ancient Egyptians stored their food and water in large ceramic jars made from clay.

40 Mud bricks used to build houses were sometimes stamped with the name of the reigning ruler.

41 Wealthy people had lush, flower-filled gardens and ponds on their estates.

42 Gardens could contain a variety of trees including sycamore, fig, pomegranate, jujube, willow, and nut trees.

43 Flowers such as daisies, cornflowers, roses, jasmine, and ivy were also common in gardens.

44 Wealthy people sweetened their food and drinks with honey from bees that they kept. Poorer people used fruit juice and dates as sweeteners.

45 To bathe, the poor would often wash themselves in the Nile River.

46 Rich homeowners had a bathing room located beside their bedroom. Servants would pour water over a person who was seated on a limestone slab.

47 People traveled long distances by boat and short distances by walking or riding donkeys.

48 Horse-drawn chariots were sometimes used by wealthy people as a form of transportation.

49 Furniture was typically made of many pieces of wood held together by pegs fitted into drilled holes.

50 DISEASE AND POOR NOURISHMENT MEANT MANY NEWBORNS IN ANCIENT EGYPT WOULDN'T SURVIVE, SO SOME PARENTS DIDN'T NAME THEIR CHILDREN UNTIL THEY WERE OLDER.

51 Many people were called by nicknames—even rulers. For example, Ramses II was nicknamed "Sisi."

52 Sometimes, a child was given a name that referred to his or her parents. For example, Satkamose translates to "daughter of Kamose."

53 Ancient Egypt was a tourist destination for some ancient Greeks and ancient Romans. Visitors often carved their names into stone as a record of their visit.

54 Ancient Egyptians themselves traveled to other regions, but for religious and business purposes.

55 Firelighters used to create fires for cooking and heat consisted of a spindle, or stick, and a block with holes drilled into it.

56 The spindle of a firelighter was placed into one of the block holes and rotated rapidly. The rubbing motion created heat and, eventually, flames.

57 Ancient Egyptians ate with their hands. They also used spoons but did not have knives or forks.

58 Hunting was a popular pastime during ancient Egypt's early years, before the area around the Nile was cultivated for farming.

59 Over time, hunting became a sport for Egypt's upper classes. To hunt, they used weapons such as spears, arrows, and throwing-sticks.

60 Fishing was also a popular pastime. Fishermen would typically stand in their canoes and spear their prey with harpoons.

61 Some women worked outside the home as managers in the linen-making industry.

62 Clothing was washed with detergents made from natural ingredients such as natron—a type of salt.

63 ANCIENT EGYPTIAN SOCIETY WAS DIVIDED INTO A CLASS SYSTEM. THERE WERE AT LEAST SIX CLASSES. UPPER-CLASS PEOPLE ENJOYED A WEALTHY LIFESTYLE WHILE THE LOWEST CLASS WAS POOR.

64 Naturally, Egypt's ruling family were at the top of the system. Below them was a class of top government officials, high priests, and nobles.

65 Other religious leaders, doctors, engineers, and writers called scribes made up the third class.

66 The fourth and fifth classes included craftsmen, soldiers, and merchants. The poorest classes included unskilled laborers, farmers, and fishermen. Only the servants and slaves ranked lower.

67 Most people remained in the same social class they were born into.

68 MOVING UP THE SOCIAL LADDER WAS POSSIBLE IF A PERSON RECEIVED AN EDUCATION OR TRAINING IN A SPECIAL SKILL— BOTH OF WHICH REQUIRED MONEY.

69 Workers—particularly those building pyramids— received free medical services from doctors.

70 Some ancient Egyptians kept an altar in their home, where they left offerings to deceased family members or gods for protection.

71 Home altars could include an inscribed stone or wooden tablet called a stela, which would offer magical protection from dangerous animals such as snakes and scorpions.

72 A stela was also used as a tombstone, to help people identify the resting place of a deceased person.

73 A large stela was sometimes used to identify city and district boundaries.

74 Ancient Egyptians collected drinking water from the Nile River or wells and stored it in large ceramic vessels.

75 Women rubbed the surfaces of the vessels with the seeds of the horseradish tree. Scientists believe these seeds helped kill harmful bacteria in the water.

sun-dried mud-brick walls

1 THE WORD "PHARAOH" COMES FROM *PER-AA*, EGYPTIAN FOR "GREAT HOUSE." IT ORIGINALLY REFERRED TO THE ROYAL PALACE BUT CAME TO MEAN "KING."

2 Around 2925 B.C. NARMER—also known as Menes—joined Upper and Lower Egypt and became the FIRST PHARAOH of a UNIFIED EGYPT.

3 Narmer called Memphis, the CAPITAL CITY of the unified kingdom, "WHITE WALLS." The name may have referred to the whitewashed walls of his castle.

4 After a pharaoh's death, the THRONE was usually passed down to his ELDEST SON.

5 NOT ALL PHARAOHS HAD ROYAL PARENTS. AY, AN ADVISER TO TUTANKHAMUN, BECAME KING AROUND 1322 B.C. AFTER TUTANKHAMUN DIED WITHOUT ANY HEIRS.

6 About 170 pharaohs ruled EGYPT. At least seven pharaohs were WOMEN, probably starting with Merneith, who ruled around 2900 B.C. Here Nefertiti is shown.

25 FABULOUS FACTS ABOUT

7 Ramses II, who became pharaoh in 1279 B.C., had artists create MANY COLOSSAL STATUES of himself. One measured 36 feet (11 m) tall.

8 RAMSES II TOLD HIS PEOPLE THAT HE HAD DEFEATED THE HITTITES, AN ENEMY OF EGYPT, WHEN IN REALITY THE BATTLE WAS A DRAW.

9 Ramses II had tales of his ALLEGED VICTORY against the Hittites engraved on monuments to PERSUADE other ENEMIES not to strike Egypt.

10 Ancient Egyptians believed that the pharaoh could COMMUNICATE WITH THE GODS and became a god after death.

11 Akhenaten, who ruled around 1353 B.C., ANGERED MANY PEOPLE by insisting they WORSHIP ONLY ONE GOD, Aten, a sun god, instead of many gods.

12 Akhenaten's obsession with Aten was likely INFLUENCED BY HIS FATHER, Amenhotep III, who also worshipped this sun god.

13 THUTMOSE IV DREAMED THAT THE GREAT SPHINX AT GIZA ASKED HIM TO CLEAR AWAY SAND DRIFTS THAT HAD NEARLY BURIED IT IN EXCHANGE FOR THE THRONE.

14 Thutmose IV became king around 1400 B.C. after his brother, a pharaoh, died. He commemorated the event by CREATING A STELA FOR THE GREAT SPHINX.

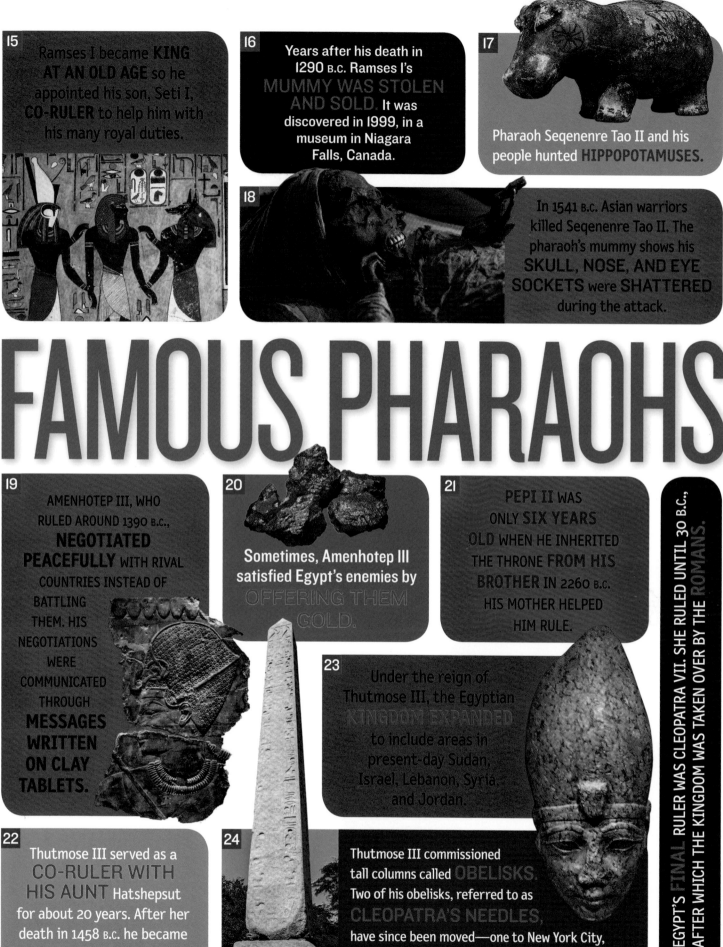

15 Ramses I became **KING AT AN OLD AGE** so he appointed his son, Seti I, **CO-RULER** to help him with his many royal duties.

16 Years after his death in 1290 B.C. Ramses I's **MUMMY WAS STOLEN AND SOLD.** It was discovered in 1999, in a museum in Niagara Falls, Canada.

17 Pharaoh Seqenenre Tao II and his people hunted **HIPPOPOTAMUSES.**

18 In 1541 B.C. Asian warriors killed Seqenenre Tao II. The pharaoh's mummy shows his **SKULL, NOSE, AND EYE SOCKETS** were **SHATTERED** during the attack.

FAMOUS PHARAOHS

19 AMENHOTEP III, WHO RULED AROUND 1390 B.C., **NEGOTIATED PEACEFULLY** WITH RIVAL COUNTRIES INSTEAD OF BATTLING THEM. HIS NEGOTIATIONS WERE COMMUNICATED THROUGH **MESSAGES WRITTEN ON CLAY TABLETS.**

20 Sometimes, Amenhotep III satisfied Egypt's enemies by OFFERING THEM GOLD.

21 PEPI II WAS ONLY **SIX YEARS OLD** WHEN HE INHERITED THE THRONE **FROM HIS BROTHER** IN 2260 B.C. HIS MOTHER HELPED HIM RULE.

22 Thutmose III served as a CO-RULER WITH HIS AUNT Hatshepsut for about 20 years. After her death in 1458 B.C. he became the sole pharaoh.

23 Under the reign of Thutmose III, the Egyptian KINGDOM EXPANDED to include areas in present-day Sudan, Israel, Lebanon, Syria, and Jordan.

24 Thutmose III commissioned tall columns called OBELISKS. Two of his obelisks, referred to as CLEOPATRA'S NEEDLES, have since been moved—one to New York City, U.S.A., and one to London, England.

25 EGYPT'S FINAL RULER WAS CLEOPATRA VII. SHE RULED UNTIL 30 B.C., AFTER WHICH THE KINGDOM WAS TAKEN OVER BY THE ROMANS.

1
When the Egyptians began embalming their dead around 3000 B.C., only pharaohs and those close to them were mummified.

2
Soon, anyone who could afford the expensive embalming process was mummified.

3
A fishing tribe called the Chinchorros, who lived in present-day Chile, mummified the dead about 2,000 years before the Egyptians.

4
The funerary mask placed over an Egyptian mummy showed the deceased person's face in an idealized, not realistic, way.

5
Royal funerary masks were made from precious metals such as gold and silver.

6
Less expensive death masks were created from cartonnage, a material made from papyrus or linen that was soaked in plaster.

7
Common people in ancient Egypt could not afford mummification so they were simply buried in the sand in cemeteries.

8
Bodies buried in sand were naturally mummified. The sand soaked up the bodies' moisture and helped to preserve them.

9
More than 1,700 mummies have been discovered buried in sand in Fag el-Gamous, a burial site south of Cairo, Egypt.

10
Embalmers mummified bodies in booths set up along the banks of the Nile.

11
In the 20th dynasty, Egyptians started inserting stones—painted to resemble eyes—under the eyelids of mummies.

12
In the early 1800s, some people in England bought mummies from Egypt and then hosted events during which they would unwrap the dead bodies to study them.

13
According to one legend, a cursed mummy aboard the *Titanic* caused the ship to sink. However, no evidence exists of a mummy on the ship.

14
The mummy of Ramses II became the first to receive a passport when it was flown from Egypt to France in 1974.

15
The Egyptian passport of Ramses II listed his job title as "king (deceased)."

16
The mummies of many Egyptian pharaohs had their arms placed across their chest.

17
Female royals who were mummified during the New Kingdom typically had their arms placed against their sides.

18
Before wrapping a mummy in linen bandages, embalmers painted on its eyebrows and hairline in black to make it look more lifelike.

19
A mummy's toes were individually wrapped to keep them from breaking off.

20
Often, fake hair coated with red plant dye, henna, was placed on the head of mummies.

21
A gel made from fatty acids of plants and animals could be used to style the mummy's hair and hold it in place.

22
One female mummy had more than 30 tattoos of baboons, cows, lotus blossoms, and other objects all over her body.

23
Scientists believe that the tattoos on the mummy's throat were intended to give her power as she sang and played music during religious rituals.

24
In the mid-1800s, an American paper manufacturer purchased Egyptian mummies so he could use their linen bandages to make paper.

25
From the 11th to the 17th centuries A.D., mummies were ground up and sold as medicine in parts of Asia and Europe.

26
After the embalmers placed a mummy inside its coffin, a funeral procession took place from the embalmers' tent to the tomb, where priests performed rituals.

27
During a funeral procession, priests, dancers, musicians, and relatives of the deceased walked alongside the coffin as it was pulled by oxen.

28
After the mummy was entombed, the funeralgoers took scraps left over from the embalming process and buried them nearby.

29
The lavish burials of wealthy ancient Egyptians attracted thieves who would raid the tombs for valuables.

30
Ancient Egyptian kings became worried about tomb robbers, so they made arrangements to have their mummies placed in hidden tombs in a valley.

31
The **Valley of the Kings**, located near Luxor, contains **63 known tombs** that housed the mummies of Thutmose I, Tutankhamun, Amenhotep II, and other pharaohs.

34
Many **mummified cats were sold as souvenirs** to tourists in the early 1800s.

37
Mummified food—including beef, duck, and pigeon—has been **discovered in some tombs.**

41
Wealthy nobles had their own burial ground, or necropolis.

46
Before 2800 B.C. a **pharaoh's servants were killed** and buried near the pharaoh so that they could continue serving in the afterlife.

32
The mummies of many ancient Egyptian queens were entombed in the nearby Valley of the Queens.

35
In A.D. 1888, an Egyptian farmer discovered more than 100,000 mummified cats buried in the sand.

38
In 2016, Egyptologists found the mummies of 50 baby crocodiles wrapped together with the mummies of two larger crocodiles.

42
Mummy portraits were likely painted near the time of death and carried during the funeral procession before the deceased was taken to the embalmer.

47
The practice of **killing servants** was replaced with the act of burying the dead with *shabtis*—figurines believed to be able to do work for the deceased in the afterlife.

33
Ancient Egyptians also **mummified family pets** and animals that represented gods.

36
After the Romans conquered ancient Egypt, a new custom of placing a **portrait of the deceased** person over his or her mummy came into fashion.

39
The mummified crocodiles, which were bound together with pine rope, were likely an **offering to Sobek, the crocodile god.**

43
Many mummy portraits were **painted on panels** made from the wood of sycamore, pine, fir, cypress, and oak trees.

48
At a necropolis known as Qubbet el-Hawa, scientists discovered a tomb with 14 **family members** of a powerful ancient Egyptian governor named Sarenput II.

44
Over time, the Egyptians discovered that dry sand could preserve a body in just 40 days.

40
In 1902, the mummy of an ordinary ancient Egyptian man named Hapi-men was discovered with his mummified dog curled at his feet.

45
In the A.D. 1800s, people traveling through Egypt sometimes used **mummies as fuel** when they ran out of firewood.

49
King Francis I of France, who reigned from A.D. 1515 to 1547, **swallowed a pinch of ground mummy each day.** He believed it would make him stronger.

50
Scientists studying a **2,400-year-old** female mummy discovered that her embalmers had accidentally left the **brain-removal tool** inside her skull.

50 Unraveled Facts About MUMMIES

Pyramids at Giza

1 Ancient Egyptians believed that DISEASES were caused by the GODS or EVIL DEMONS inhabiting the body.

2 As well as giving a patient medicines, DOCTORS of the time often PERFORMED SPELLS to rid the body of the evil force attacking it.

3 To SOOTHE COUGHS, DOCTORS prepared a concoction made from figs, dates, anise, honey, and water.

4 Treatment for a BROKEN NOSE was similar to the procedure done today. The person's nose was BANDAGED AND ROLLS OF LINEN were placed inside the nostrils.

5 Ancient Egyptians CHEWED ON SAND PARTICLES that were accidentally in flour used to make bread. The grains WORE DOWN THE ENAMEL AND MADE CAVITIES IN THEIR TEETH.

25 MEDICINAL FACTS ABOUT DISEASES

6 Egyptian dentists FILLED CAVITIES WITH CEMENT or a mixture of tree sap and minerals.

7 A WOOD-AND-LEATHER TOE on an ancient Egyptian mummy found near Luxor shows that they used PROSTHETIC DEVICES for missing limbs.

8 Doctors in ancient Egypt treated people who had suffered a CROCODILE BITE—and survived—by BANDAGING THEIR WOUNDS WITH FRESH MEAT.

9 To treat a SNAKEBITE, doctors used a knife to cut the flesh around the infected area and then POURED SALT over the wound.

10 HEADACHES WERE TREATED BY RUBBING THE HEAD WITH A FRIED CATFISH.

11 Imhotep was a famous architect and doctor. His medical skills were so respected that he was made a god 1,200 YEARS AFTER HIS DEATH.

12 DOCTORS STITCHED UP DEEP GASHES WITH BONE OR COPPER NEEDLES AND STRIPS OF LINEN.

13 According to one ancient Egyptian MEDICAL RECORD, if a skull has been fractured and the brain exposed, it should be treated with a SPRINKLING OF OIL.

14 SURGERY was performed to treat WOUNDS on the body's surface, and aids such as CRUTCHES were used for injuries.

15 THE ROOTS OF WATER LILIES WERE PRESCRIBED FOR A VARIETY OF AILMENTS, INCLUDING RASHES, SORES, AND STOMACHACHES.

16 Some ancient Egyptians were victims of the CANAL-DWELLING SCHISTOSOME WORM, which enters the body through the legs or feet and can damage a person's liver.

17 THE EGYPTIANS WERE ALSO AFFECTED BY GUINEA WORMS—PARASITES THAT ENTER THE BODY THROUGH DRINKING WATER AND LAY EGGS, MAKING THEIR HOSTS ILL.

18 Many ancient Egyptian CHILDREN SUFFERED FROM ANEMIA, a blood disease often caused by a LOW-IRON DIET.

AND CURES

19 WEALTHY EGYPTIANS could afford MEAT, which is high in fat content. As a result, many people in the upper classes SUFFERED FROM HEART DISEASE.

20 Windblown SAND AND DIRT GRAINS sometimes got caught under people's eyelids causing EYE INFECTIONS.

21 The mummy of RAMSES I has a misshapen ear—a condition experts believe was caused by a SEVERE EAR INFECTION that led to the pharaoh's death in 1290 B.C.

22 ANCIENT EGYPTIANS TREATED BURNS, RASHES, AND CUTS WITH ALOE VERA, A PLANT THAT IS STILL USED TODAY TO TREAT SOME SKIN CONDITIONS.

23 BLACKFLIES were known to spread a disease that BLINDED ANCIENT EGYPTIANS. Since blackflies breed in the Nile River, the disease is known as "RIVER BLINDNESS."

24 Ancient Egyptian doctors treated BLINDNESS BY MASHING UP A PIG'S EYE WITH RED CLAY and pouring the mixture into a patient's ear.

25 ANCIENT EGYPTIAN EYE MAKEUP was made of materials such as a galena—a lead-based substance that ACTED AS MEDICINE and helped combat eye infections.

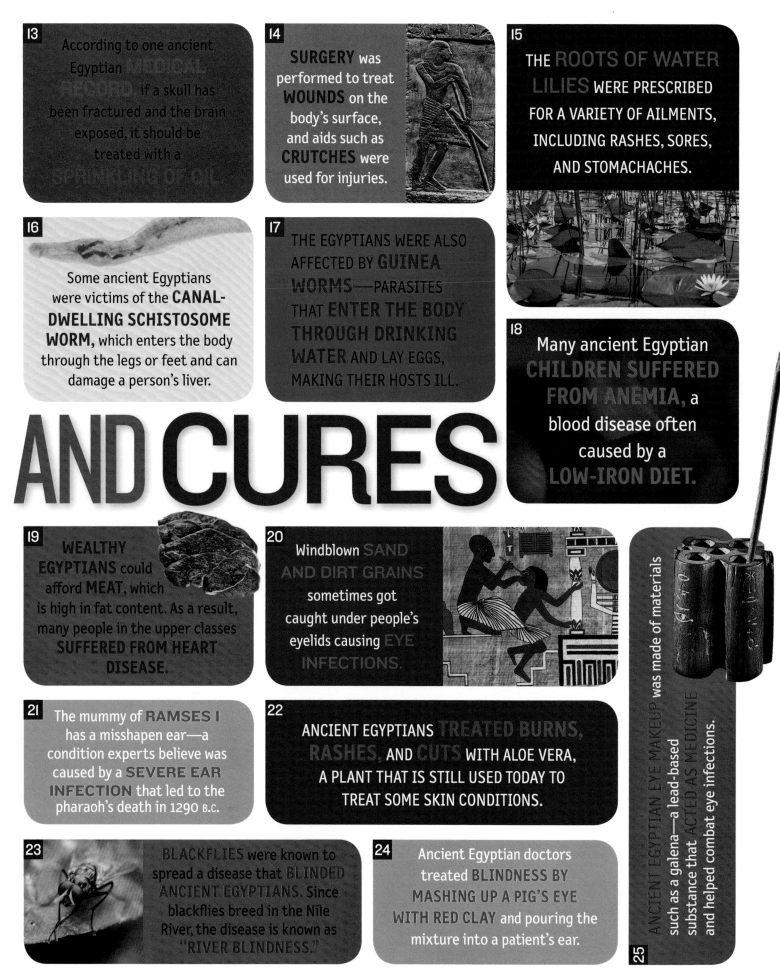

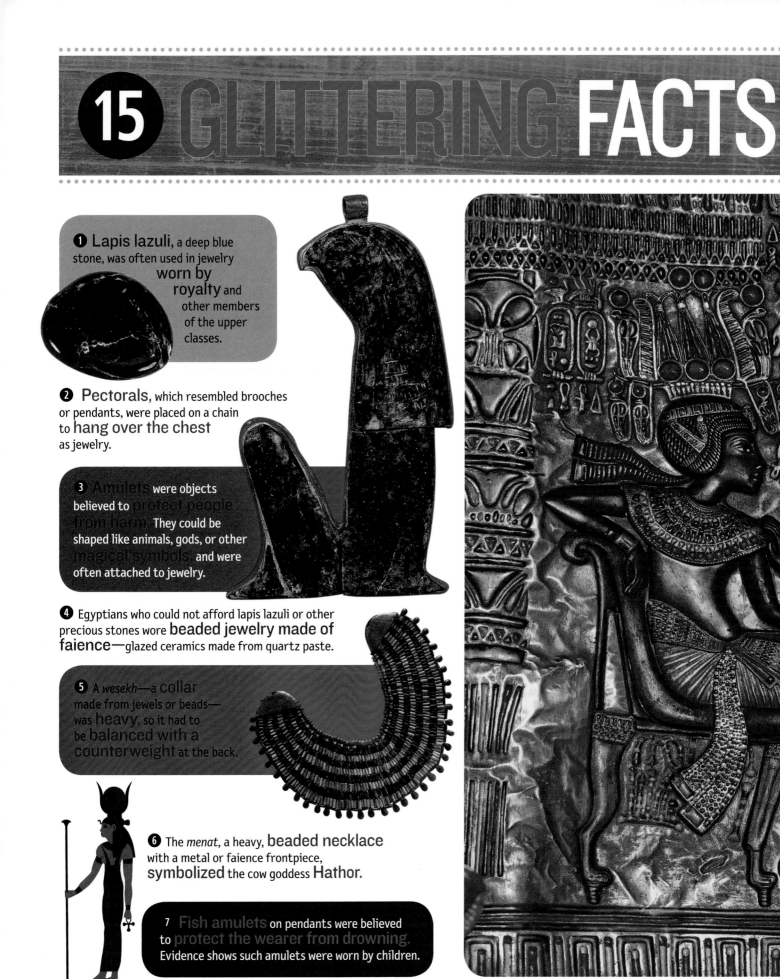

1 Lapis lazuli, a deep blue stone, was often used in jewelry **worn by royalty** and other members of the upper classes.

2 Pectorals, which resembled brooches or pendants, were placed on a chain to **hang over the chest** as jewelry.

3 Amulets were objects believed to protect people from harm. They could be shaped like animals, gods, or other magical symbols and were often attached to jewelry.

4 Egyptians who could not afford lapis lazuli or other precious stones wore **beaded jewelry made of faience**—glazed ceramics made from quartz paste.

5 A *wesekh*—a **collar** made from jewels or beads—was **heavy**, so it had to **be balanced with a counterweight** at the back.

6 The *menat*, a heavy, **beaded necklace** with a metal or faience frontpiece, **symbolized** the cow goddess **Hathor**.

7 Fish amulets on pendants were believed to **protect the wearer from drowning.** Evidence shows such amulets were worn by children.

ABOUT JEWELRY

8 Scarab beetles, associated with the sun god, became a popular symbol used in pendants, bracelets, rings, and other jewelry.

9 Gold, which was mined in the Eastern Desert, was believed to be the flesh of the sun god, Ra.

10 Gold was stored in treasuries attached to some temples. Records of the amount of gold delivered to these temples were kept by the pharaoh.

11 Gold signet rings had the names and titles of their wearers engraved into them.

12 Signet rings were used like signatures. The wearer would pour molten wax on a document and press the ring into the wax to leave a distinctive mark.

13 Ancient Egyptians mined a light-blue mineral called turquoise in the Sinai Peninsula.

14 The ruler Cleopatra VII was particularly fond of emeralds and often presented them as gifts to foreign officials.

15 The scarcity of silver in ancient Egypt made this precious metal highly valued for jewelry. Sometimes, it was more sought after than gold.

King Tutankhamun and Queen Ankhesenamun wearing *wesekh* collars

1 Although most ancient Egyptian rulers were male, **SOME WOMEN DID RULE**—particularly when a male ruler was too young to take the throne.

2 Around 1539 B.C., 10-year-old AHMOSE inherited the throne. Since he was too young to lead Egypt, HIS MOTHER, AHHOTEP, ruled until he turned 16.

3 The EGYPTIANS PRAISED AHHOTEP for looking after soldiers, encouraging them to fight after a defeat, and eventually bringing peace to Egypt.

4 After Ahhotep died, Ahmose honored his mother by placing a necklace with fly pendants in her tomb.

5 Experts once doubted that MERNEITH—Egypt's FIRST FEMALE PHARAOH—was a ruler, but in 1985 her name was discovered on an ancient seal listing Egypt's leaders.

25 FASCINATING FACTS ABOUT

6 According to one tale, the female ruler NITOCRIS, who reigned from 2184 to 2181 B.C., MURDERED HER BROTHER'S ASSASSINS at a banquet.

7 NEFERTITI, whose name means "the beautiful woman has come," was known for her GREAT BEAUTY. She was married to the PHARAOH AKHENATEN.

8 Various artworks of the time depict Nefertiti as her husband's equal. She is often shown striking EGYPT'S ENEMIES and even wearing the PHARAOH'S CROWN.

9 After Aten was declared Egypt's main god, Nefertiti changed her name to NEFERNEFERUATEN, meaning "Aten is the most beautiful, Nefertiti."

10 Nefertiti was TUTANKHAMUN'S STEPMOTHER. Tutankhamun's BURIAL MASK may have been originally created for Nefertiti.

11 After Amenemhet IV died around 1760 B.C., there was NO MALE TO TAKE THE THRONE so his half sister, SOBEKNEFRU, became pharaoh of Egypt.

12 SOBEKNEFRU, WHOSE NAME HONORS SOBEK, THE CROCODILE GOD, ESTABLISHED A RELIGIOUS AND ECONOMIC CENTER IN FAIYUM, A CITY WHERE CROCODILES WERE WORSHIPPED.

13 Sobeknefru's portraits often show her wearing a STRIPED ROYAL HEADCLOTH and BELTED SKIRT—clothing usually worn by men.

14 While mostly royal women married pharaohs, a commoner named TIYE married Amenhotep III (1390 to 1353 B.C.). Tiye became an important figure in the ROYAL COURT.

15 Unlike previous queens, Tiye's NAME was ENGRAVED with her husband's name on official monuments.

16 Tiye identified with the cow goddess, HATHOR, and was the first queen to wear Hathor's HEADDRESS, which consisted of horns and a sun disk.

17 BASED ON THE TEMPLE AND ELABORATE TOMB THAT RAMSES II BUILT FOR HIS WIFE, QUEEN NEFERTARI, EXPERTS BELIEVE SHE WAS HIGHLY RESPECTED BY HIM.

FEMALE RULERS

18 A pair of MUMMY'S LEGS discovered in Nefertari's tomb are believed to be the LIMBS of the late queen, who died around 1250 B.C.

19 QUEEN CLEOPATRA II revolted against her husband—and brother—Ptolemy VIII, when he demanded a DIVORCE and married her daughter from a previous marriage.

20 THE GREEKS WHO LIVED IN PARTS OF UPPER EGYPT SUPPORTED CLEOPATRA II, SO SHE BECAME THEIR SOLE RULER UNTIL HER DEATH IN 116 B.C.

21 CLEOPATRA VII—made famous by her portrayal in MODERN MOVIES AND BOOKS—became Egypt's ruler in 51 B.C., along with her young brother Ptolemy XIII.

22 With the help of JULIUS CAESAR, a Roman ruler, Cleopatra VII DEFEATED HER BROTHER and took over Egypt.

23 ALTHOUGH CLEOPATRA VII RULED EGYPT, SHE WAS OF GREEK DESCENT.

24 After Caesar's death, Cleopatra joined forces with Roman general Mark Antony to OVERTHROW ROME'S NEW RULER, Octavian.

25 According to one legend, Cleopatra killed herself with a BITE FROM A VENOMOUS SNAKE after she heard that Mark Antony had died in battle.

1 In ancient Egypt, workers were usually **paid with food.** Scribes were among the top earners, receiving about **seven sacks of grain** per month.

men and women harvesting grain

2 **Brickmakers** made bricks by mixing Nile mud with sand, straw, and water, and pouring the mixture into brick molds.

3 **Mourners** were people who were **paid to grieve for someone who had died.** They would beat their chests and wail loudly at funerals.

4 **Coffinmakers** offered customers several options. For budget-conscious Egyptians, **coffins** made of clay were the affordable choice, while wealthy Egyptians chose more expensive **timber coffins.**

5 **Jewelry makers** had various tasks. For example, some **bore holes into beads and stones** with bow drills, while others **threaded the ornaments on papyrus string.**

6 A **royal sandal bearer** was a top official whose responsibility was to **carry the pharaoh's sandals** while guarding him or her.

7 **Linen** was produced in **large workshops** throughout ancient Egypt. Many women served as **overseers, or managers,** of these fabric workshops.

8 **Temporary workers** who were hired to help **build the pyramids** were likely paid **10 loaves of bread** each day to feed their families.

9 **Merchants** could work for the king or queen or the temples. They traveled to nearby regions and **traded** Egyptian products for animal skins, minerals, and other goods.

10 Similar to doctors today, doctors in ancient Egypt were trained in specific areas of the body. Some focused on the head, others treated internal problems, and some specialized in the eyes.

11 Some **women became doctors.** Lady Peseshet, who lived around 2500 B.C., was Egypt's first known female physician.

12 **Barbers** carried tools such as **scissors, razors,** and **styling lotions** in decorative cases when they made house calls to wealthy Egyptians.

13 **Supervisors** were hired to **manage pyramid workers.** They split the men into groups and assigned them different tasks, such as moving materials or decorating tombs.

14 Goldsmiths transformed natural gold into thin sheets that were used to gild furniture, weapons, jewelry, and sarcophagi.

15 **Teachers** were usually **temple priests or government officials.**

1 Ancient Egyptian DOG BREEDS were similar to modern-day GREYHOUNDS, MASTIFFS, BASENJIS, and SALUKIS.

2 Ancient Egyptians had MANY DIFFERENT PETS, including cats, dogs, monkeys, gazelles, and geese.

3 Egyptian dogs wore collars and had NAMES, some of which translate to BLACKIE, SPOT, GOOD SHEPHERD, and NORTH WIND.

4 One GUARD DOG, named Abuwtiyuw, was placed in HIS OWN TOMB after he died.

5 Ancient Egyptians MOURNED the death of their pet cats by SHAVING THEIR EYEBROWS.

25 BEASTLY FACTS ABOUT ANIMALS

6 Cats were prized pets because of their ASSOCIATION WITH THE CAT GODDESS Bastet and their ability to PROTECT FOOD from rats, mice, and snakes.

7 Ancient Egyptian cats were similar to modern-day TABBY CATS.

8 Pigs and boars were sometimes feared because they were associated with the violent god Seth.

9 The WHITE IBIS was associated with THOTH, the god of writing. The bird was used as a hieroglyphic symbol for Thoth.

10 PIECES OF FABRIC depicting IBISES were sometimes sewn onto the linen BANDAGES OF IBIS MUMMIES.

11 THE HIPPOPOTAMUS ONCE THRIVED IN THE NILE AND POSED A DANGER TO BOATS AND TO PEOPLE WORKING ALONG THE RIVER'S BANKS.

12 Narmer, the king who unified Egypt, was supposedly KILLED BY A HIPPOPOTAMUS.

13 THE ANCIENT EGYPTIAN BOOK OF THE DEAD CONTAINED A SPELL TO WARD OFF COCKROACHES.

14 IVORY RODS with images of animals such as crocodiles and lions were used as "MAGIC WANDS" to ward off evil.

15 A STORY FROM ANCIENT EGYPT TELLS OF A MAN WHO TRANSFORMED A WAX CROCODILE INTO A REAL ONE TO KILL AN ENEMY. CROCODILES WERE OFTEN MUMMIFIED.

16 Baboons ARE VERY vocal during sunrise, SO ANCIENT EGYPTIANS ASSOCIATED THEM WITH THE SUN GOD.

17 WHILE SOME EVIDENCE OF CAMELS IN ANCIENT EGYPT EXISTS, THE ANIMALS DID NOT BECOME A MODE OF TRANSPORTATION THERE UNTIL ABOUT 525 B.C.

18 DONKEYS were used for TRANSPORTATION and to carry HEAVY LOADS.

IN EGYPT

19 The SCARAB BEETLE was a popular insect that was known to collect animal dung, roll it into a ball, and lay its eggs inside.

20 Ancient Egyptians believed that the scarab beetle ROLLED THE SUN ACROSS THE SKY, and they associated the insect with the sun god.

21 Any one of several venomous snakes might attack ancient Egyptians working in the fields or in their homes. Death from snake-bites was quite common.

22 ROYAL CROWNS sometimes featured a GOLDEN COBRA. The cobra was depicted with its hood raised, ready to strike, as if to PROTECT THE PHARAOH.

23 During TIMES OF FLOODING, many FROGS would appear on the Nile's muddy banks. Flooding provided water for crops, so FROGS became a SYMBOL OF ABUNDANCE.

24 The most widespread SCORPION in ancient Egypt was probably the venomous DEATHSTALKER species. Egyptians used "magic spells" to treat its stings.

25 The ELECTRIC CATFISH, which can release an electrical charge to shock its enemies, would sometimes zap fishermen using catch nets along the Nile.

1 During the **Beautiful Feast of the Valley,** ancient Egyptians **honored the dead** by sailing to the Nile's west bank, where they visited temples and tombs.

2 During the **Wag Festival,** people **wore floral collars and visited chapels** to leave offerings for those who had entered the afterlife.

3 A **robed statue of the god Amun** was paraded through each town during the Festival of Opet so that people **could ask him for help.**

4 To **honor Osiris,** many ancient Egyptians used **corn and grain to make Osiris mummy figures,** which they buried in sacred locations.

5 Important dates in a pharaoh's life were sometimes carved in stone for people to remember. They included the dates of the pharaoh's coronation and marriage.

6 After the pharaoh **Amenhotep I** died, a **four-day festival** was established to remember his achievements and honor him.

7 Ancient Egyptians celebrated their new year, called Wepet Renpet, with large feasts.

8 Pharaohs **kept a record of festivals, completion of buildings,** and other important events by recording them on **temple walls** or on **stelae.**

9 During the **Heb Sed,** or the **Sed Festival,** a pharaoh who **ruled for about 30 years** would run around a field with objects that represented his right to rule Egypt.

10 Heb Sed was often commemorated with stone carvings that showed the pharaoh running beside a bull to prove his fitness to rule.

11 When a **pharaoh died,** the kingdom went into a **mourning period** that lasted 70 days. During this time, all **feasts and festivals were strictly prohibited.**

12 Ancient Egyptians in Thebes **constructed a boat** and carried it around a temple during the Henu Festival, which honored Sokar, a god of funerary crafts and tomb builders.

13 To honor the **god Bes,** protector of households, people paraded through towns **wearing masks of the god,** while musicians and dancers performed.

14 Ancient Egyptians **led a cow,** or cow statue, **covered in black linen** through streets to commemorate the legend of **Isis grieving** for her dead husband.

15 During **celebrations that honored Isis,** Egyptians **built temporary shrines** using shrubs and reeds and decorated them with flowers.

a singer plays a musical instrument before the god Re-Horakhty

45

1
Most experts believe that agriculture in ancient Egypt began in the delta region, a fertile area where the Nile fans out into the Mediterranean Sea.

2
In ancient Egypt, floodwaters of the Nile deposited mineral-rich particles called silt on the river's banks, making the land fertile for farming.

3
Silt is created over thousands of years as the Nile's rushing waters grind mineral-rich rocks, boulders, pebbles, and stones against each other.

4
Ancient Egyptians discovered that the Nile flooded each year from June to September, and developed their crop-growing season around it.

5
Some ancient Egyptian farmers rented the land they farmed from temples, the government, and wealthy landowners.

6
Wealthy landowners rarely farmed their own land. They usually hired peasant farmers to do the job for them.

7
Ancient Egyptians directed the Nile's floodwater inland by digging long irrigation canals, or channels, in the earth.

8
Ancient Egyptians attempted to build a dam across the Nile to help control flooding, but the construction was destroyed by a rush of water.

9
Today the Nile's floodwaters are controlled largely by the Aswan Dam, which was built in the 1960s.

10
The flood levels of the Nile were not consistent each year. Sometimes, the water level was too low, which resulted in poor harvests.

11
Ancient Egyptians used a *shaduf*—a pole with a bucket on one end and a weight on the other—to move water from the Nile to irrigation canals.

12
Before the invention of the shaduf, Egyptians collected water in pots and then poured it into the canals.

13
Eventually, ancient Egyptians began using a waterwheel called a *sakia* to deliver water from the river.

14
As sakias rotated, the pots attached to them collected water and poured it into irrigation canals.

15
Plows were pulled by oxen, which were leased to farmers by temples or the government.

16
The seeds for crops came from the previous year's harvest and were given to farmers by the government.

17
Farmers directed animals such as goats or oxen to walk across the sown fields and push the seeds into the ground.

18
Farmers made up about 80 percent of ancient Egypt's population.

19
After the harvest season, farmers were drafted by the government to perform various duties, such as digging canals and surveying the land.

20
Ancient Egyptians grew so much grain that the ancient Romans thought of Egypt as "the breadbasket of the world."

21
Crops were harvested from March to April, just before Egypt's temperatures would rise and make it impossible for plants to grow without sufficient water.

22
To cut the grain, early farmers used sickles with blades made from sharpened wood.

23
After the grain was cut, it was bundled and then carried by donkeys to a dry storage area called a granary, which was usually controlled by the government.

24
Some granaries were shaped like beehives, while others were square structures with flat roofs and steps along the side.

25
Shrines were sometimes built around granaries to honor Renenutet, a snake goddess who the Egyptians believed nurtured their crops.

26
Farmers sometimes had hoofed animals, such as donkeys or oxen, walk over wheat and barley to thresh it, or to separate the grains from their husks.

27
Later, farmers used a threshing sledge to separate grain from husks. The sledge had a wooden frame fitted with stone or metal teeth.

28
An animal would pull the sledge in a circular pattern over heaps of wheat or barley on the ground.

29
To keep insects and other pests away from their grain storage, ancient Egyptians used items such as bird fat and burnt gazelle dung.

30
In early ancient Egypt, women ground grain into flour with a stone that resembled a rolling pin.

31
Over time, flour production became a large industry. Men placed the grain into large limestone bowls and ground it with long wooden poles.

35
The limbs of fig trees are too weak to hold the weight of a person, so ancient Egyptians trained monkeys to climb up and collect the fruit.

39
Egyptian farmers relied on slingshots to chase away birds from their crops.

43
Flowers such as cornflowers, chrysanthemums, and lotuses were also grown in gardens and used to make bouquets.

47
Hatshepsut, who ruled from 1473 to 1458 B.C., organized trips to foreign lands to bring living trees such as myrrh to Egypt.

32
Granaries usually had a separate room for scribes, who would keep records of the amount of grain collected.

36
Sycamore figs, which were introduced to Egypt around 3000 B.C., can ripen only if they are pollinated by a wasp called *Ceratosolen arabicus*.

40
Grapes used to make wine were mostly grown in an oasis, or small fertile area surrounding a water source, in the Western Desert.

44
Droppings collected from bird shelters were likely used as fertilizer in gardens.

48
Sometimes children were stationed in the fields to scare away birds and voles to prevent the animals from eating the crops.

49
Farmers were responsible for providing food for ancient Egypt's military—which had as many as 40,000 troops.

50 Plowed-Up Facts About FARMING

33
At harvesttimes musicians sometimes went into the fields and played songs to help farmers keep a rhythm as they cut the grain.

37
The *Ceratosolen arabicus* wasp was introduced to Egypt long after the sycamore fig tree began growing there, so in ancient times the figs were seedless and dropped to the ground unripened.

41
The first fruits and crops collected during the harvest season were usually given to temples and dedicated to the gods.

45
Insect-eating birds were protected by the government of ancient Egypt because they fed on pests that would otherwise destroy crops.

50
Today, Egypt continues to grow grain, fruits, and vegetables, but its most important crop is cotton— which it sells to other countries.

34
Ancient Egyptians grew many fruits to eat including dates, grapes, figs, plums, melons, and pomegranates.

38
Eventually, ancient Egyptians discovered that scraping or bruising the sycamore figs caused them to ripen before falling to the ground.

42
Wealthy people in ancient Egypt often had private gardens, where they grew vegetables such as garlic, onions, and radishes.

46
Some rulers were eager to bring non-native plants to Egypt. For example, Thutmose III had irises brought to Egypt from present-day Syria.

1 BASKETMAKING was an early ancient Egyptian tradition. Baskets that are more than 7,000 YEARS OLD have been discovered in the Nile region.

2 Baskets were usually WOVEN FROM THE LEAVES of palm trees.

3 MANY BASKETS WERE DECORATED WITH GEOMETRIC PATTERNS SUCH AS SQUARES, WHILE OTHERS FEATURED ANIMAL DESIGNS.

4 ANCIENT EGYPTIANS BEGAN MAKING **PAPYRUS,** A PAPERLIKE WRITING MATERIAL, AROUND 3000 B.C. IT WAS THEIR MOST POPULAR WRITING MATERIAL FOR ALMOST 4,000 YEARS.

5 The paper was made from the pith, or central part, of PAPYRUS STALKS. The pith was cut into strips, which were then pressed flat and dried.

6 **Black ink** WAS MADE BY BURNING NATURAL MATERIALS SUCH AS WOOD, GRINDING THE ASHES, AND THEN MIXING THEM WITH WATER AND PLANT GUM.

25 CRAFTY FACTS ABOUT

7 COLORFUL PIGMENTS— used to paint pictures on tomb walls—were made by GRINDING MINERALS. For example, ochre was used for yellow and iron ore for red.

8 The color we now call EGYPTIAN BLUE was created by HEATING ingredients such as COPPER, natron SALT, and SAND made from quartz.

9 Ancient Egyptian PAINTINGS depicted EVERYDAY LIFE, the GODS, the AFTERLIFE, and the KING, among other things.

10 The most SIGNIFICANT PERSON OR DEITY of a painting was usually drawn very large to emphasize their importance.

11 ARTISTS POSED FIGURES IN CERTAIN WAYS TO SHOW EMOTIONS. FOR EXAMPLE, PEOPLE IN MOURNING WERE DRAWN WITH THEIR PALMS TURNED TOWARD THE FACE.

12 Ancient Egyptians believed that a STATUE HELD THE SPIRIT of the dead person it depicted.

13 CRAFTSPEOPLE made WOODEN MODELS of everyday scenes that were often planted in tombs for use by the deceased in the afterlife.

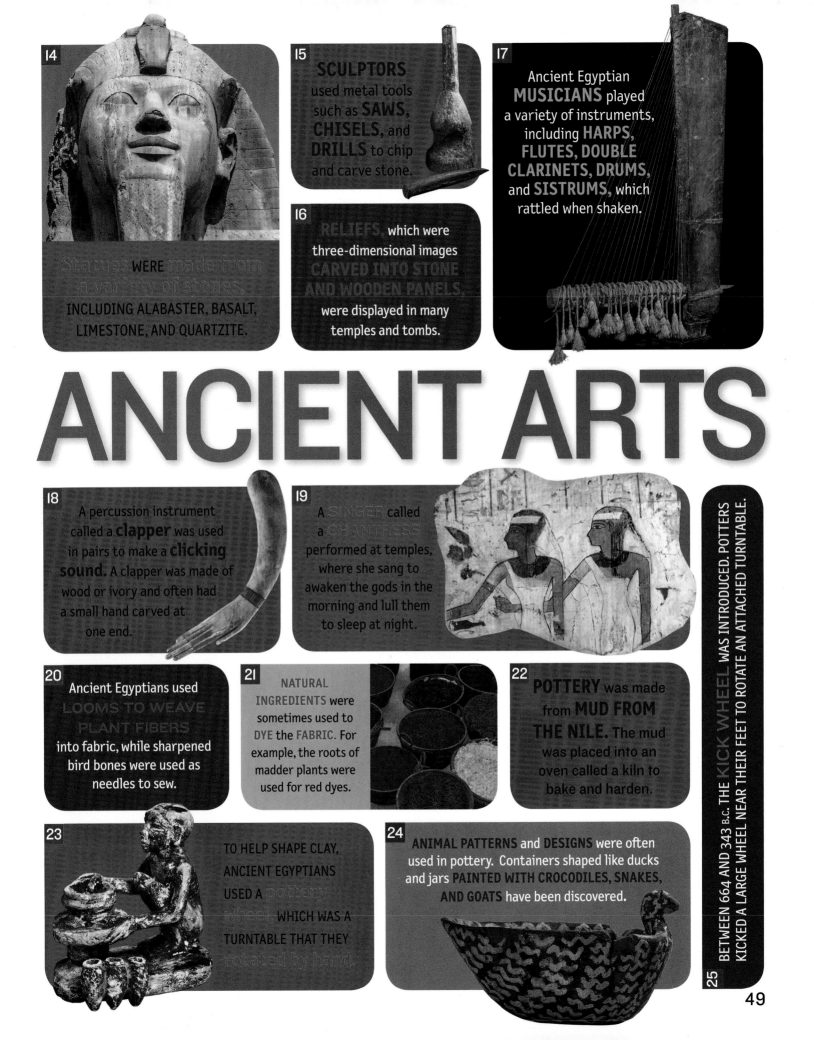

14 Statues WERE made from a variety of stones, INCLUDING ALABASTER, BASALT, LIMESTONE, AND QUARTZITE.

15 SCULPTORS used metal tools such as SAWS, CHISELS, and DRILLS to chip and carve stone.

16 RELIEFS, which were three-dimensional images CARVED INTO STONE AND WOODEN PANELS, were displayed in many temples and tombs.

17 Ancient Egyptian MUSICIANS played a variety of instruments, including HARPS, FLUTES, DOUBLE CLARINETS, DRUMS, and SISTRUMS, which rattled when shaken.

ANCIENT ARTS

18 A percussion instrument called a **clapper** was used in pairs to make a **clicking sound.** A clapper was made of wood or ivory and often had a small hand carved at one end.

19 A SINGER called a CHANTRESS performed at temples, where she sang to awaken the gods in the morning and lull them to sleep at night.

20 Ancient Egyptians used LOOMS TO WEAVE PLANT FIBERS into fabric, while sharpened bird bones were used as needles to sew.

21 NATURAL INGREDIENTS were sometimes used to DYE the FABRIC. For example, the roots of madder plants were used for red dyes.

22 POTTERY was made from MUD FROM THE NILE. The mud was placed into an oven called a kiln to bake and harden.

23 TO HELP SHAPE CLAY, ANCIENT EGYPTIANS USED A pottery wheel, WHICH WAS A TURNTABLE THAT THEY rotated by hand.

24 ANIMAL PATTERNS and DESIGNS were often used in pottery. Containers shaped like ducks and jars PAINTED WITH CROCODILES, SNAKES, AND GOATS have been discovered.

25 BETWEEN 664 AND 343 B.C. THE KICK WHEEL WAS INTRODUCED. POTTERS KICKED A LARGE WHEEL NEAR THEIR FEET TO ROTATE AN ATTACHED TURNTABLE.

49

❶ About 4,000 years ago the Egyptians **created a lock** that would help people **open a barred door** from the outside.

❷ Ancient **Egyptian locks had pegs** that held the crossbar in place. When a key was inserted into the lock, the pegs lifted and unlocked the door.

❸ To fight bad breath, ancient Egyptians created **breath mints.** The mints were pellets **made by boiling spices** such as cinnamon, frankincense, or myrrh with honey.

❹ The Egyptians had their own version of deodorant, made from the chocolate-scented pods of the carob plant.

❺ The Egyptians developed a paste to clean their teeth around 1550 B.C. The **toothpaste was made from mineral powder, clay, and honey.**

❻ Between 3500 and 3000 B.C. ancient Egyptians— and Babylonians—created **toothbrushes** by **fraying the ends of twigs.**

❼ Ancient Egyptians were the first to put **papyrus** to good use, utilizing it to make **paper, boats, beds, floor mats, wall coverings, ropes, baskets,** and **sandals.**

❽ Ancient Egyptians invented workshops and gangs, or teams, of craftspeople so they could mass-produce boats and farming equipment and construct palaces and pyramids.

a carpenters' workshop

ABOUT INVENTIONS

9 Ancient Egyptians made round **hand mirrors** from flattened sheets of metal that were polished until they were reflective. A **decorated handle** was fixed to the metal.

10 The oldest known **baby rattles** appeared in ancient Egypt around 1400 B.C. The rattles were made from clay or wood and **filled with pebbles.**

11 Ancient Egyptians may have been the first people to bake sourdough bread.

12 The first known **umbrellas** appeared in ancient Egypt. These umbrellas were **held over pharaohs to emphasize their power** and to protect them from the hot sun.

13 Ancient Egyptian mummy makers were the first people known to use **stitches.** Their stitches were **made from plant fiber, hair, and wool thread.**

14 **Marshmallows** may have originated in ancient Egypt. People squeezed sap from mallow plants and mixed it with nuts and honey to make their version of the treat.

15 Today's barbers are using a tool probably invented in ancient Egypt. Early Egyptians fitted sharp stone—and later, copper—blades to wooden handles to make razors.

1 Ancient Egypt's **GOVERNMENT** was divided into three main branches—**CIVIL, RELIGIOUS,** and **MILITARY.**

2 Since ancient Egyptians believed the **PHARAOH** had been chosen by the gods, he or she was given **COMPLETE CONTROL** of the government.

3 THE PHARAOH APPOINTED AN OFFICIAL CALLED A VIZIER, OR CHIEF OVERSEER, TO HELP RUN THE GOVERNMENT.

4 The **vizier** met regularly with government officials and **reported information** back to the pharaoh.

5 Sometime before 2575 B.C. the pharaoh divided ancient Egypt into **42 DISTRICTS CALLED NOMES.**

25 POLITICAL FACTS ABOUT

6 EACH NOME HAD A GOVERNOR CALLED A NOMARCH, WHO WAS APPOINTED BY THE PHARAOH.

7 Each nome FUNCTIONED LIKE A SMALL GOVERNMENT. It had its own treasury, capital, temples, court, army, and even its own god.

8 During ancient Egypt's early years **viziers** were selected from the royal family, but eventually **common people could be chosen** for the role.

9 Viziers wore a LONG ROBE that extended to the ankles and a chain around the neck with an AMULET SYMBOLIZING TRUTH AND JUSTICE.

10 AS ANCIENT EGYPT BECAME WEALTHIER, MORE TEMPLES WERE BUILT AND THE INFLUENCE OF INCREASED. BY 1353 B.C. THEY IN POWER.

11 At the height of their power, priests claimed **ONLY THEY COULD INTERPRET THE WILL OF THE GODS,** and the pharaoh had to follow their orders.

12 Only people who could SPEAK WELL PUBLICLY could address the king and his officials. Others had to remain silent.

13 When Akhenaten became pharaoh around 1353 B.C., HE TOOK POWER AWAY FROM THE PRIESTS by changing ancient Egypt's religion.

14 To diminish the role of priests, Akhenaten declared there was only ONE GOD instead of many and that ONLY HE COULD INTERPRET THE GOD'S WILL.

15 Most government officials inherited their positions from relatives, but AMENHOTEP II, who ruled from 1426 to 1400 B.C., APPOINTED HIS CHILDHOOD FRIENDS to these jobs.

16 All government OFFICIALS WERE ABLE TO READ and were considered scribes.

17 During the 6th dynasty, King Pepi I's mother-in-law, NEBET, served as a vizier. She is the first known woman in ancient Egypt to hold the title.

GOVERNMENT

18 WOMEN were legally considered EQUAL TO MEN. They were allowed to represent their husbands in business matters.

19 From 1550 B.C. onward, the KING'S WIFE was given the title of "God's Wife of Amun" and was REQUIRED TO SERVE AS A HIGH PRIESTESS in temples.

20 In this role, the QUEEN WAS GIVEN PROPERTIES, where she would organize religious events and services.

21 The God's Wife of Amun had a STAFF THAT REPORTED TO HER. The staff included a SCRIBE for counting grain and an OVERSEER OF CATTLE.

22 A CHANCELLOR managed all the affairs of the palace. This included everything from finances to hiring tutors to educate the royal children.

23 THE KING'S DUTIES INCLUDED DECIDING THE PUNISHMENT OF PEOPLE FOUND GUILTY IN COURT.

24 During ancient Egypt's early years, high officials GREETED THE KING BY KISSING HIS FEET.

25 There was no COINED MONEY in ancient Egypt until the 30th dynasty. Government taxes were paid as quantities of GRAIN, MEAT, LEATHER, or days of MANUAL WORK.

❶ **Workers ate two meals each day.** For breakfast, they had bread and soft onions, and for dinner they ate broiled vegetables, meat, and more bread.

❷ Since Egypt's hot climate caused fish to spoil quickly, they were preserved by being salted, pickled, or dried in the sun.

❸ **Preserving fish** was such an important task in ancient Egyptian society that it was often the **responsibility of temple officials.**

❹ Bread—a staple of the ancient Egyptian diet—was **baked in molds** that came in a **variety of shapes,** including round, oval, pyramid, and crescent.

bakers mixing and kneading bread dough

❺ In 1996 an archaeologist re-created an **ancient Egyptian bread recipe** that used **emmer wheat.** She described the bread as **rich, sweet,** and **tasty.**

❻ Ancient Egyptians flavored their food with spices such as anise, cumin, and cinnamon, and with herbs such as fenugreek, dill, and coriander.

❼ **Cows, goats, and donkeys** provided ancient Egyptians with **milk.**

❽ Ancient Egyptian workers trampled grapes with their bare feet in large vats to make wine.

9 It is believed that the **average ancient Egyptian adult** ate at least **3,780 calories each day.** That's equal to the calories in seven Big Macs.

10 To cook, ancient Egyptians used **oils extracted from the seeds** of moringa and sesame plants.

11 **Raw cabbage,** which was grown in many gardens, was often served as an **appetizer** before meals.

12 Ancient Egyptians enjoyed eating fruits such as dates, figs, melon, lotus blossom, and doum—a fruit that grows on a type of palm tree.

13 Ancient Egyptians used sheep and goat milk to make **cottage cheese, butter,** and **cream.**

14 **Wealthy people** hosted **banquets** where expensive foods such as **grilled bull, roasted goose,** and **baskets of fruit** were served.

15 Ancient Egyptians **raised bees for honey.** They made beehives from dried mud and stored honey they collected in clay jars.

1 Temples in ancient Egypt were [built to honor a particular god]. In fact, the ancient Egyptian word for temple was *hwt-ntr*, meaning "house of god."

7 The temple built by Amenhotep III was called the "House of Millions of Years"—most likely because ancient Egyptians expected the temple to last that long.

13 [Common people] could enter the [temple's courtyard] but they were not allowed inside the sanctuary.

19 Records show that Karnak had 433 orchards, 421,000 livestock, 65 villages, and 83 ships.

25 Tall, tapering pillars called [obelisks] were often placed in front of temples. The obelisks were either a [tribute to the gods] or [to commemorate] an important event.

2 [Early temples] were made of [mud bricks], but by 2650 B.C. builders [switched to stone], which lasted much longer.

8 Once fully built, the House of Millions of Years stretched 1,968 feet (600 m) in length. That's longer than 20 basketball courts.

14 Temples were important to ancient Egyptian kings because each provided a place for the king to interact with a specific god.

20 Many ancient Egyptian temples had rows of tall columns that supported a roof. This was called hypostyle architecture.

26 Obelisks were often cut from stone in quarries and transported to the temples by boats along the Nile.

3 Temples functioned like small towns. They had [homes, storage areas], [libraries], and even [schools].

9 Archaeologists digging at the site of Amenhotep III's temple found 600 statues of the goddess Sekhmet. Ancient records state there were 730 originally.

15 [Paintings] show the kings offering gifts to and dressing statues inside the sanctuaries, but these rituals were actually performed by priests.

21 It is believed that new rulers were crowned on the grounds of Karnak in a building now called the Great Hypostyle Hall.

27 Unlike most temples, which were dedicated to one god, [a temple] in southern Egypt was dedicated to two: [Sobek], the crocodile god, and [Horus] the falcon god.

4 Giant stone statues of kings were often erected in front of temples. The statues were large to make the king seem godlike.

10 Amenhotep III's temple was destroyed after his death by an earthquake. Later pharaohs collected materials from the ruins to build their own temples.

16 Karnak is a giant ancient temple complex in Luxor, Egypt, that spans more than 247 acres (100 ha). That's large enough to hold 187 football fields.

22 To celebrate the construction of a new temple, small objects that featured the king's name were buried in the building's foundation.

28 Experts believe temple priests raised crocodiles in Kom Ombo. Many crocodile mummies have been found at the site.

5 Temple builders likely used [levers and ramps] to move stones and make carvings on temple stones.

11 Most ancient Egyptian temples had a courtyard and a room called a sanctuary, where a statue of the temple's god was placed.

17 It took more than [100 years to build Karnak]. About 28 different rulers contributed to its construction.

23 The entryway to most temples was fronted with two trapezoid-shaped towers called pylons.

29 [Mortuary temples] were buildings that [honored dead pharaohs]. They were sometimes built alongside pyramids.

6 The Colossi of Memnon stand 75 feet (23 m) tall. These two giant statues were part of a temple built by King Amenhotep III 3,400 years ago.

12 The sanctuary was usually a dark room made of wood and gilded gold.

18 Karnak was built to honor the creator god, Amun-Re. The Egyptians believed the god lived in Karnak with his wife, Mut, and their son, Khonsu.

24 Colorful flags representing gods were often hoisted on tall masts located above the temple's pylons.

30 Ramses II began construction on his mortuary temple, the Ramesseum, shortly after he came to the throne in 1279 B.C. It took 22 years to complete.

31
When it was finished, the Ramesseum had several buildings and a seated statue of Ramses II that measured 57 feet (17.4 m) tall.

32
Ramses III commissioned a mortuary temple where people would worship him after he died. The temple was built in a complex called Medinet Habu.

33
The Luxor Temple was connected to Karnak by a long row of sphinxes—mythical creatures with a king's head and a lion's body.

34
Statues of Amun-Re and his family were carried from Karnak to the Luxor Temple during the Festival of Opet to refresh the pharaoh's power.

The was built between 237 and 57 B.C. to honor

36
The Edfu Temple is one of Egypt's best preserved temples because it was buried by sand. Archaeologists unearthed the temple in the 1800s.

The remains of a temple dedicated to a who was believed to have created humans from clay on a potter's wheel, were discovered on

38
Sometimes temples were targeted by thieves. Between 1156 and 1145 B.C., a priest stole a sacred amulet and cattle from the Temple of Khnum at Elephantine.

39
The island of Philae in southern Egypt was home to several temples. One of these was a complex built for Isis, the goddess of magic and the heavens.

40
The Temple of Isis features 59-foot (18-m)-tall columns and a small chapel dedicated to her son, Horus.

41
After the Aswan Dam was built in the 1960s, the island of Philae became flooded and its temples were in danger of being ruined.

42
To save the temples of Philae from floodwaters, experts cut them into 50,000 pieces and moved them to nearby Agilika Island, where they were reassembled.

Queen Hatshepsut's temple

Between 1279 and 1213 B.C., had in located on the west bank of the Nile.

44
The larger of the two temples in Abu Simbel was dedicated to Ramses II himself. Four statues created in the king's likeness guarded the entryway.

45
The Great Temple of Ramses II was built such that sunlight would shine into the entryway on October 22 and February 22—likely the dates of the king's birth and coronation.

46
Scenes decorating the temple walls feature Ramses II in battle, firing arrows from a chariot.

47
The smaller of the two temples in Abu Simbel was likely built for Queen Nefertari, who was married to Ramses II.

48
The Temple of Nefertari features two statues of the queen and four of Ramses II. Each statue stands between supports decorated with hieroglyphs.

49
The temples of Abu Simbel—like those of Philae—were threatened by floodwaters after the Aswan Dam was built, and therefore had to be moved.

50
It took about 3,000 workers five years to cut Ramses II's temples from the mountain and move them to high desert land 600 feet (183 m) from the original site.

50 Towering Facts About the TEMPLES

15 INSPIRATIONAL

1 Unlike true ancient Egyptian obelisks, which are carved from one massive block of stone, the Washington Monument in Washington, D.C., is made from more than 36,000 stone blocks.

2 Temple Works, a former company building in Leeds, England, was designed to look like the Temple of Horus at Edfu. The company produced linen—an Egyptian specialty.

3 The Egyptian Theatre in DeKalb, Illinois, U.S.A., was built in 1928 in the ancient Egyptian Revival style.

4 Two cast-iron sphinxes are placed at each end of the Egyptian Bridge in St. Petersburg, Russia.

5 Four glass-and-metal pyramids mark the entrance to the Louvre Museum in Paris, France. The largest is made of 673 panes of glass.

6 In 2015, officials in Egypt announced plans to build a pyramid-shaped skyscraper. The Zayed Crystal Spark tower will stand 656 feet (200 m) when completed.

7 The glass pyramids in the Muttart Conservatory—a botanical garden in Edmonton, Alberta, Canada—are not just for show. They serve as greenhouses for many flowers.

8 An obelisk in Rugby, North Dakota, U.S.A., marks the geographic center of North America. The tower is made from local rocks, including fieldstone and granite.

the largest glass pyramid in the center of the Louvre Museum, Paris, France

ANCIENT EGYPTIAN DESIGN

9 Following **Emperor Napoleon's conquest** of Egypt in 1801, ancient Egyptian decorative art became popular in France. **Styles of Egyptian art** were copied by architects and theater designers.

10 The **Luxor Hotel** in Las Vegas, Nevada, U.S.A., is a 350-foot (107-m)-tall **pyramid** with a **giant sphinx** statue. The hotel once had an **artificial Nile River!**

11 **Harrods,** a store in London, England, introduced the **Egyptian Hall** in the 1990s. It includes a statue of an Egyptian king, cartouches, and Egyptian art.

12 The Passage du Caire in Paris, France, is a passageway that features **stone figures** of the cow goddess, **Hathor.**

13 **Lenin's Tomb** in Moscow, Russia, holds the mummy of former Soviet leader Vladimir Lenin. The tomb design was inspired by King Djoser's Step Pyramid.

14 The **Gold Pyramid House** in Wadsworth, Illinois, U.S.A., was built as a **family home** in 1977. A **giant statue of Ramses II** stands guard over the house.

15 **LEGOLAND** in Billund, Denmark, features a model of Egypt's **Abu Simbel Temple** made from 265,000 Lego pieces.

1 After his father died in 1479 B.C., THUTMOSE III WAS TOO YOUNG TO BE KING so his stepmother, HATSHEPSUT, BECAME HIS CO-RULER.

2 At the beginning of her reign, Hatshepsut GAVE HERSELF THE THRONE NAME MAATKARE, which means "truthful is the spirit of Ra." The name was used in her CARTOUCHE.

3 Although her subjects knew she was female, HATSHEPSUT WORE MALE CLOTHING AND A ROYAL FALSE BEARD to help them accept her as a king.

4 Hatshepsut often had artists include something to reveal her gender, such as her real name, which means "FOREMOST OF THE NOBLE WOMEN."

5 Hatshepsut claimed the SUN GOD, AMUN-RE, SAID SHE WAS DESTINED TO BE KING. This story is inscribed on a chapel in Hatshepsut's temple.

25 HEROIC FACTS ABOUT

6 Hatshepsut had four large obelisks created for Karnak Temple. It took 27 boats manned by 850 oarsmen to transport these obelisks.

7 Hatshepsut's TEMPLE, DJESER-DJESERU, which has THREE COLUMNED TERRACES, IS built into the BASE OF A CLIFF in western Thebes.

8 The walls of Djeser-Djeseru are DECORATED WITH SCENES THAT SHOW FESTIVALS that took place in the temple and other EVENTS IN HATSHEPSUT'S LIFE.

9 Hatshepsut's REIGN WAS A PEACEFUL ONE for Egypt. The Egyptian army FOUGHT ONLY ONE BATTLE—with the Nubians to the south—and won.

12 THE EGYPTIANS filled five ships WITH A VARIETY OF LUXURY GOODS FROM PUNT. THESE GOODS INCLUDED gold, ivory, apes, and myrrh trees.

10 Hatshepsut organized a successful trade expedition to the LOST KINGDOM OF PUNT, located near the Red Sea.

11 The expedition was the first time in 500 years that an ancient Egyptian had visited Punt, a region they called "THE LAND OF THE GODS."

13 According to an Egyptian official named Djehuty, **HATSHEPSUT HERSELF FOUGHT IN THE BATTLE AGAINST NUBIA.**

14 Hatshepsut awarded her most **TRUSTWORTHY OFFICIAL, SENEMUT, 93 TITLES,** including the great steward of Amun, which placed him in charge of Karnak Temple's business matters.

15 At least **25 STATUES** of Senemut were commissioned. He was also buried in a quartzite sarcophagus usually reserved for royalty.

16 AT **HER DEATH** AROUND 1458 B.C., HATSHEPSUT HAD **RULED EGYPT** FOR ABOUT **20 YEARS.**

17 Hatshepsut's **STEPSON, THUTMOSE III,** became the sole ruler of Egypt after her death. For unknown reasons, he HAD MANY OF HER MONUMENTS DESTROYED.

18 Hatshepsut was buried in a tomb in the Valley of the Kings, but sometime after her burial, **HER MUMMY VANISHED.**

HATSHEPSUT

19 In the A.D. 1800s, a canopic chest labeled with **HATSHEPSUT'S CARTOUCHE** was discovered. It contained the organs of a mummy.

20 In the early 1900s, an unknown mummy was discovered. Archaeologists noticed that its left arm was placed over its chest in a **ROYAL BURIAL POSE** and thought it might be Hatshepsut.

21 Scientists scanned Hatshepsut's canopic chest and discovered it contained one of the ruler's **MOLAR TEETH.**

22 After measuring the **MOLAR,** scientists realized it **COULD FIT PERFECTLY IN THE MOUTH** of the unknown mummy, which they concluded was Hatshepsut.

23 SCANS OF HATSHEPSUT'S MUMMY REVEAL THAT SHE HAD CANCER AND DIABETES AND MAY HAVE DIED FROM A CONDITION RESULTING FROM A TOOTH INFECTION.

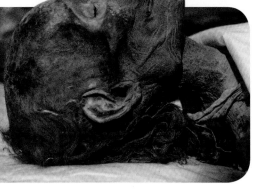

24 ANOTHER MUMMY was originally discovered alongside Hatshepsut. It was Sitre-In, A WOMAN WHO HAD NURSED Hatshepsut as a baby.

25 STONE BLOCKS DEPICTING HATSHEPSUT were discovered on Elephantine Island. They may have been part of a structure intended as a station for boats CARRYING SPIRITS IN THE AFTERLIFE.

15 FUN FACTS ABOUT

1 Animal knucklebones were sometimes carved into animal shapes and used as **playing pieces**.

2 To play a **board game** called **twenty squares**, the Egyptians moved cone- and spool-shaped playing pieces across a board while **trying to capture their opponent's pieces**.

3 Ancient Egyptian children played with **spinning tops made from clay, wood, or stone**. They pulled a whip wrapped around the top to make it spin.

4 A **wooden toy cat** with bronze teeth was discovered in Thebes. A piece of string running through the toy cat's mouth could be pulled to **open and shut its jaws**.

5 A **popular board game** called *senet* required players to roll knucklebones and then move their playing pieces along rows of squares in a race to the finish.

6 King **Tutankhamun** was a fan of senet. **Four senet board games** were discovered in his tomb.

7 Some children's toys were made with **movable parts**. Pulling a string could work a **lever to lift an object** or it could **close** an animal's jaws.

8 In the ancient Egyptian version of **tug-of-war**, children on either side of the center line clutched each other **around the waist** while those at opposite ends pulled them.

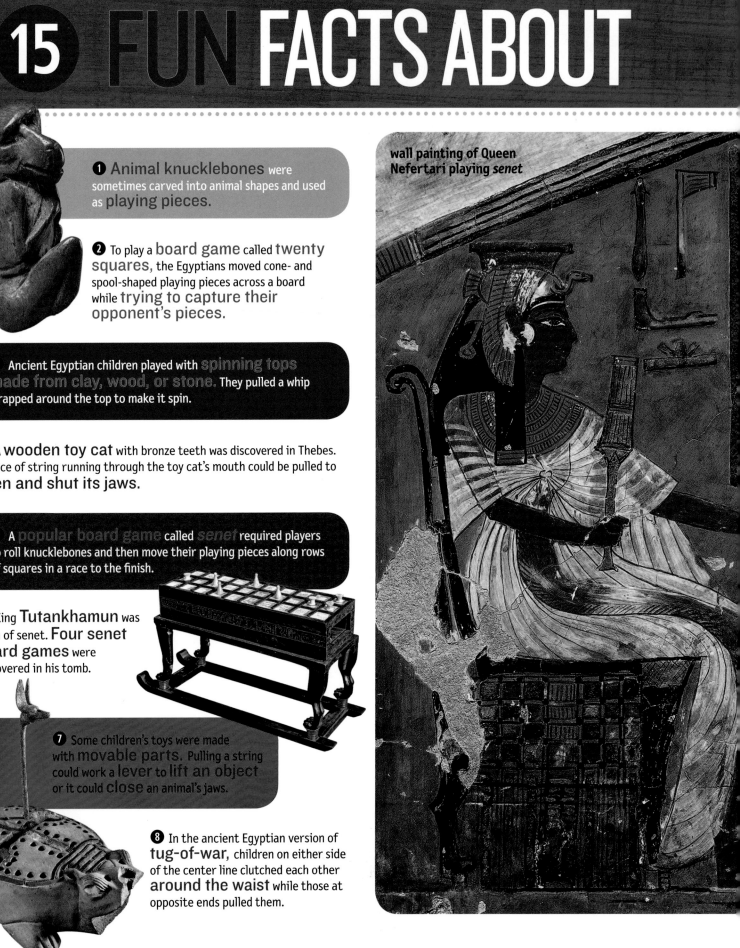

wall painting of Queen Nefertari playing *senet*

GAMES AND PASTIMES

9 *Mehen,* or the "snake game," was played on a **game board designed to resemble a coiled snake.** Playing pieces were of various shapes, including lions.

10 Ancient Egyptian kings performed a game called *seker-hemat* that is **similar to modern-day baseball.** The kings batted a ball while priests acted as catchers.

11 Tomb-wall drawings in the ancient city of Memphis show the Egyptians playing handball. Since the balls were made of flimsy materials, such as plant fibers or hay, they likely only lasted one match.

12 **Boat jousting** was played on canoes. Paddlers steered canoes toward each other while men **tried to knock one another off with long sticks.**

13 The ancient Egyptian game hounds and jackals may have been similar to Chutes and Ladders. It was played on a violin-shaped game board with dog- and jackal-shaped pegs.

14 Ancient Egyptian **children played** a version of **leap-frog** in which they hopped over a seated person, who tried to trip them in the process.

15 Some gaming disks featured animal carvings. When the disks were spun, the animals appeared to chase one another.

15 SELLABLE FACTS ABOUT

❶ Before coined money was introduced, **Egyptians exchanged goods,** such as barley, for other food and household items.

❷ Ancient Egyptian merchants used **metal weights** to **determine prices.** Goods were placed on balancing scales and weighed against metals such as gold, silver, and copper.

❸ The *deben* was a **unit used for pricing** goods and services. A dress was worth 5 deben, while a donkey was worth 30 deben.

4 A tomb worker's monthly labor was worth 11 deben. As payment, he received five and a half sacks of grain, which was worth the same amount.

❺ Traveling to other kingdoms took time, so Egyptian merchants set up **trading posts along the Nile** where they met merchants from other kingdoms.

6 Trade wasn't conducted only within ancient Egypt. Many merchants traveled to other kingdoms, such as in Nubia in the south, where they traded stone and pottery for items such as gold, ivory, and ostrich feathers.

❼ One ancient Egyptian **trading post in Nubia had 578 storage pits** that held various goods for trade—including oil and wine.

wooden model of farmers' cattle being counted

8 Egypt's native trees did not supply high-quality wood for building, so ancient Egyptians **traded goods for cedar with the Byblos people** from present-day Lebanon.

9 Although ancient Egyptian merchants did not ride donkeys, they used the animals to carry goods when trading over land.

10 Animals such as **horses and water buffalo** were not native to ancient Egypt but were **imported from other areas** outside the kingdom.

11 **Merchants from Asia** traveled to ancient Egypt to trade their **silver, wine, and oil** for papyrus, grain, and salt.

12 The **items exchanged during** a trade were usually recorded on papyrus or "notepads" made from flakes of limestone.

13 Pharaoh Ahmose II welcomed Greek traders and even allowed them to settle in Egypt.

14 The **first known coin** minted in Egypt was struck around 360 B.C. It was likely used to **pay Greek workers** living in Egypt.

15 Greek traders living in Egypt may have been the **first people to** introduce coined money to Egypt.

1 Ancient Egyptian kings lived in MUD-BRICK PALACES that had IMAGES OF WILDLIFE painted on the floors and walls.

2 MALKATA PALACE in Thebes—built in the 1300s B.C.—was about half the size of BUCKINGHAM PALACE in London, England.

3 EACH BRICK used to build Malkata Palace WAS STAMPED WITH THE NAME OF THE KING.

9 Royal students sometimes WROTE ON WOODEN BOARDS covered in plaster that could be wiped clean and used again.

10 ROYAL TEACHERS were usually selected from MEMBERS OF THE KING'S COURT, including viziers, military leaders, and scribes.

16 PHARAOHS WORE HEADCLOTHS such as the *nemes* headdress, which was made of striped linen fabric and tied at the back.

17 During RELIGIOUS OCCASIONS, the pharaoh sat on a BLOCK THRONE that was box-shaped and had a low back.

23 Pharaohs had PETS. Amenhotep II was believed to have had a pet LION, three MONKEYS, and a DOG.

24 Before 2030 B.C. pharaohs RARELY ACCOMPANIED THEIR TROOPS into battle. They appointed military officials to lead the soldiers.

25 Egyptian texts suggest that Pharaohs THUTMOSE III and RAMSES II were WARRIORS who fought alongside their soldiers.

statue of Ramses II at Luxor

35 REGAL FACTS ABOUT

4 Royal palaces employed people who did the pharaoh's LAUNDRY. They had titles such as "CHIEF BLEACHER."

5 Visitors from other lands sometimes brought ANIMALS to the pharaoh AS GIFTS. These included monkeys, giraffes, and bears.

6 The CHILDREN OF THE PHARAOH were TAUGHT in a *kap*, or ROYAL NURSERY, at the rear of the palace.

7 Sometimes the children of important officials were ALLOWED TO ATTEND SCHOOL WITH the PHARAOH'S CHILDREN.

8 Like most students, ROYAL CHILDREN were taught WRITING, READING, and MATH, as well as good manners and honesty.

11 ROYAL NURSES were responsible for FEEDING ROYAL BABIES when the mothers could not.

12 ROYAL NURSES were so respected that some went on to MARRY TOP OFFICIALS or were BURIED WITH KINGS.

13 Pharaohs were linked with the FALCON GOD, HORUS, whose father, the god Osiris, was considered the first king of Egypt.

14 Some TEMPLE WALLS had a *serekh*—a RECTANGULAR carving bearing the RULER'S NAME and a FALCON representing Horus.

15 Pharaohs and their families stood on a balcony—the WINDOW OF APPEARANCE— at public ceremonies.

18 For NONRELIGIOUS EVENTS, the pharaoh used an ELABORATE THRONE decorated with images of lions.

19 While sitting on a THRONE, the pharaoh rested his feet on a FOOTREST decorated with images of Egypt's ENEMIES.

20 Each ancient Egyptian palace had its own BAKERY where up to 5,000 LOAVES of bread were baked every few days.

21 A scene in the tomb of Ramses III shows that servants KNEADED BREAD DOUGH BY STEPPING ON IT.

22 The pharaoh was ENTERTAINED by MUSICIANS, DANCERS, and STORYTELLERS who told tales of the gods, ghosts, and adventure.

26 The KING'S THRONE was placed on a DECORATED PLATFORM called a dais, which likely had steps leading up to the throne.

27 The dais of Ramses II was decorated with SCULPTURES OF LIONS BITING the HEADS OF EGYPT'S PRISONERS.

28 OFFICIALS who visited the king risked being beaten if they TOUCHED HIM without permission.

29 The king was sometimes CARRIED IN A PALANQUIN, a boxlike seat that had two poles on each side for bearers to hold.

30 The OVERSEER OF WIGS was responsible for managing a TEAM OF WIGMAKERS who worked at the palace.

31 Kings were allowed to marry many women, but only ONE WIFE HELD THE TITLE OF GREAT ROYAL WIFE.

32 The great royal wife could LIVE WITH THE KING, TRAVEL with him, and PERFORM SONGS for the temple gods.

33 Ancient Egyptian kings COMMUNICATED WITH THE GODS. Many kings claimed the gods gave them orders in dreams.

34 SENWOSRET I claimed GODS CAME TO HIM IN A DREAM and demanded he build a temple on Elephantine Island.

35 Later rulers CONSULTED ORACLES— which were either statues of gods or priests channeling gods— for advice.

ROYAL LIFE

1 The discovery of King Tutankhamun's tomb in 1922 sparked a worldwide craze called Tutmania. Egyptian-inspired movies, posters, and books became popular.

Howard Carter and an assistant inspect the golden sarcophagus of Tutankhamun.

2 The Kane Chronicles, a series of books by Rick Riordan, revolves around two siblings who are the descendants of two pharaohs, Narmer and Ramses II.

3 Yugi Mutou, the main character in the Japanese manga series Yu-Gi-Oh!, solves an ancient puzzle that releases the spirit of a fictional pharaoh named Atem.

4 In the 2014 movie *Mr. Peabody & Sherman,* the main characters travel back in time to ancient Egypt, where they meet King Tutankhamun.

5 One of the most famous movies released during Tutmania was *The Mummy,* in 1932.

BORIS KARLOFF (FRANKENSTEIN)
"The MUMMY"
with ZITA JOHANN
David Manners · Edward Van Sloan · Arthur Byron

6 The mummy of Imhotep—the famous Egyptian vizier, doctor, and architect—is brought to life in the classic movie *The Mummy.*

7 U.S. president Herbert Hoover named his dog King Tut.

8 "Walk Like an Egyptian," a 1986 song performed by the pop band **The Bangles,** was partly inspired by the stance of Egyptian characters in tomb drawings.

ANCIENT EGYPT

9 The 2009 movie *Night at the Museum: Battle of the Smithsonian* features ancient Egyptian Kahmunrah, who tries to steal a tablet that can bring evil historical leaders to life.

10 In **Secret of the Tomb,** a 2014 sequel to *Night at the Museum,* it is revealed that Pharaoh Ahkmenrah's father had a **high priest create the magical tablet** to keep his family together after death.

11 Prince Khufu is a fictional character in the comic book series *Hawkman.* In the series, Khufu develops superpowers from aliens that land in ancient Egypt.

12 In the animated TV show **Tutenstein,** which aired from 2003 to 2007, the mummy of a **10-year-old pharaoh** who is brought to life by a lightning bolt must learn to live in the modern world.

13 It is believed that the Pokémon character Lucario is based on Anubis, the Egyptian god of the dead who has the head of a jackal.

14 The original story of the X-Men takes place in ancient Egypt, where the villain Apocalypse is aided by the vizier Ozymandias, the Greek name for Ramses II.

15 In the 1981 movie *Raiders of the Lost Ark,* archaeologist Indiana Jones looks for—and finds—the biblical Ark of the Covenant at Tanis, a one-time capital city of ancient Egypt, in the Nile Delta.

1 Ancient Egyptians NEEDED A WAY TO KEEP RECORDS, so they developed a system of writing using characters called HIEROGLYPHS.

2 The **OLDEST KNOWN HIEROGLYPHS** were discovered in Abydos, Egypt, on pottery vessels and labels that are more than **5,000 YEARS OLD.**

3 The hieroglyphs on the labels provided information about the **QUANTITY** and **ORIGIN** of goods inside the vessels.

4 Ancient Egyptians called hieroglyphs *MDW NTR*, which means "speech of the god."

5 Some ancient Egyptian words are written with one hieroglyph that DEPICTS THE WORD. For example, the hieroglyph for "sun" is a picture of the sun.

6 Other hieroglyphs REPRESENT SINGLE LETTERS. For example, an owl was used for the letter M.

25 HANDY FACTS ABOUT

7 ANCIENT EGYPTIANS DID NOT USE PUNCTUATION OR SPACES IN BETWEEN THEIR SYMBOLS.

8 FOR SOME PLURAL NOUNS, a HIEROGLYPH WAS REPEATED. FOR EXAMPLE, THE HIEROGLYPH FOR "GOD"—A FLAG—IS REPEATED THREE TIMES TO CONVEY "GODS."

9 The **NAMES OF RULERS** were written in oval circles called **CARTOUCHES.**

10 SCRIBES were people who LEARNED TO READ AND WRITE. They were responsible for recording daily activities, writing contracts, and keeping records.

11 To write, a scribe would dip a REED PEN or SMALL BRUSH made from a stick and plant fibers into a POT OF PIGMENT.

12 The writing was usually done on papyrus, writing boards, or *ostraca*, which were pieces of pottery or flakes of limestone.

13 The hieroglyph for "scribe" showed a rectangular PALETTE for the pigment, a BRUSH, and a WATER POT.

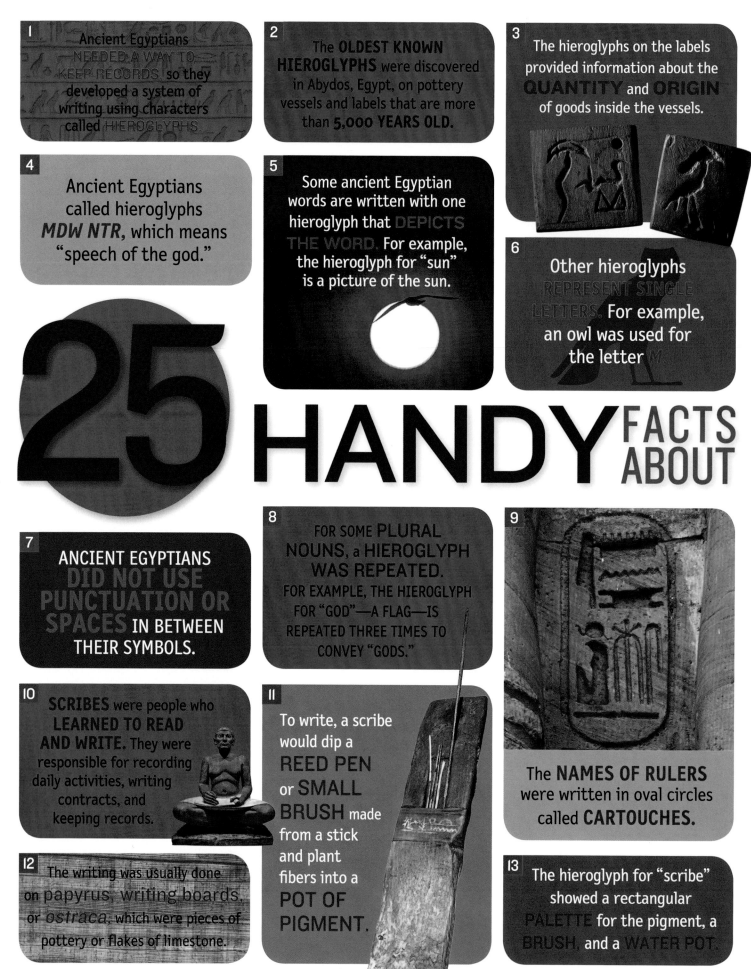

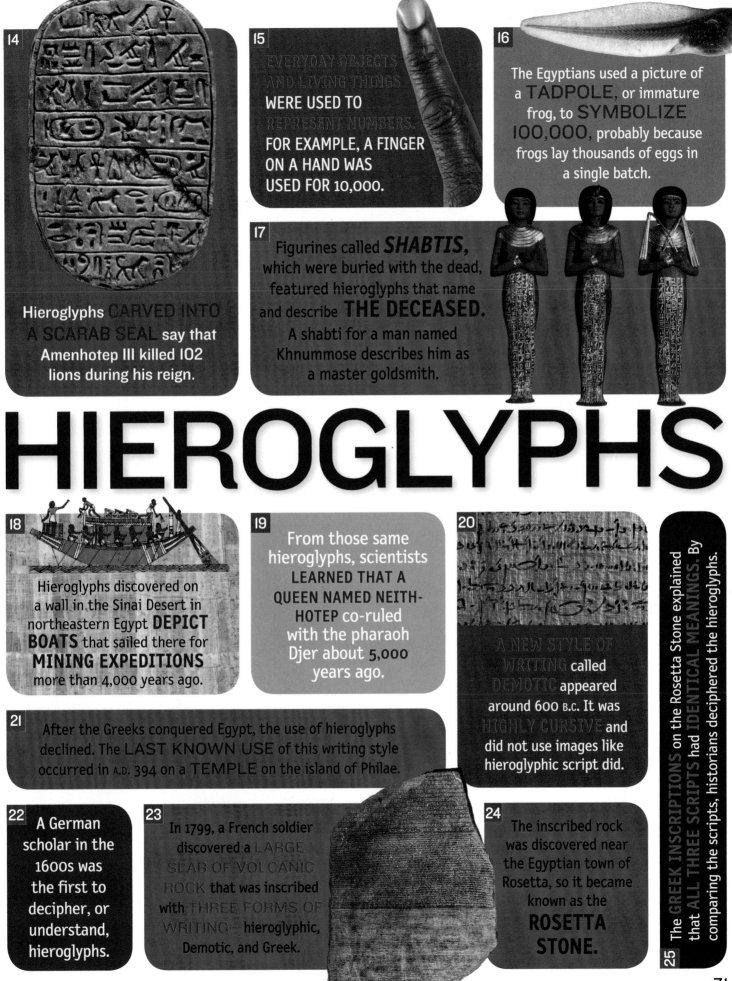

14 Hieroglyphs CARVED INTO A SCARAB SEAL say that Amenhotep III killed 102 lions during his reign.

15 EVERYDAY OBJECTS AND LIVING THINGS WERE USED TO REPRESENT NUMBERS. FOR EXAMPLE, A FINGER ON A HAND WAS USED FOR 10,000.

16 The Egyptians used a picture of a TADPOLE, or immature frog, to SYMBOLIZE 100,000, probably because frogs lay thousands of eggs in a single batch.

17 Figurines called *SHABTIS*, which were buried with the dead, featured hieroglyphs that name and describe **THE DECEASED.** A shabti for a man named Khnummose describes him as a master goldsmith.

HIEROGLYPHS

18 Hieroglyphs discovered on a wall in the Sinai Desert in northeastern Egypt **DEPICT BOATS** that sailed there for **MINING EXPEDITIONS** more than 4,000 years ago.

19 From those same hieroglyphs, scientists **LEARNED THAT A QUEEN NAMED NEITH-HOTEP** co-ruled with the pharaoh Djer about 5,000 years ago.

20 A NEW STYLE OF WRITING called DEMOTIC appeared around 600 B.C. It was HIGHLY CURSIVE and did not use images like hieroglyphic script did.

21 After the Greeks conquered Egypt, the use of hieroglyphs declined. The LAST KNOWN USE of this writing style occurred in A.D. 394 on a TEMPLE on the island of Philae.

22 A German scholar in the 1600s was the first to decipher, or understand, hieroglyphs.

23 In 1799, a French soldier discovered a LARGE SLAB OF VOLCANIC ROCK that was inscribed with THREE FORMS OF WRITING — hieroglyphic, Demotic, and Greek.

24 The inscribed rock was discovered near the Egyptian town of Rosetta, so it became known as the **ROSETTA STONE.**

25 The GREEK INSCRIPTIONS on the Rosetta Stone explained that ALL THREE SCRIPTS had IDENTICAL MEANINGS. By comparing the scripts, historians deciphered the hieroglyphs.

1 Girls often had their hair arranged in a ponytail or pigtails, but they occasionally sported a shaven head with a long side lock.

2 Young boys had shaven heads except for a lock of hair on one side. This side lock was often braided.

3 A lotion made from beeswax or resin—a plant sap—was used to style hair.

4 To protect themselves from lice and the sun's rays, wealthy men and women shaved their heads and wore wigs.

5 Wigs like this man's were made from the hair of humans and of sheep and horses. These hairs were often combined with plant fibers.

6 Wig hair was usually braided or curled, but sometimes the two styles were used in combination.

7 Perfume was made from many different ingredients, including saffron oil, cinnamon, bitter almonds, sandlewood, and iris flowers.

ANCIENT BEAUTY

women wearing perfumed cones on their wigs

8 Wealthy ancient Egyptians sported **manicured finger-nails.** The royal palace even had manicurists on staff.

9 Both ancient Egyptian **men and women used a black eyeliner called kohl** around their eyes because it helped reduce the sun's glare.

10 **To make kohl eyeliner,** the Egyptians crushed a lead-based substance called **galena** and ingredients such as ground pearls, emeralds, herbs, and fat.

11 Cosmetics such as kohl and perfume were usually stored in small stone pots.

12 **Green eye paints** made from **malachite**—an ore of copper—were applied to the eyelids.

13 **Red ochre**—an ore of iron—was rubbed on the cheeks as **blush** or was mixed with fat and **used as lip gloss.**

14 **Henna,** a red pigment that comes from the leaves of the henna plant, was **used to tint fingernails, toenails, and hair.**

15 Wax cones with scented herbs and spices may have been worn on wigs to produce a pleasant smell.

1 During ancient Egypt's early years SOLDIERS DID NOT WEAR ARMOR. Instead they wore a linen kilt and belt over a triangular loincloth.

2 EARLY SHIELDS were made of a rectangular WOODEN FRAME and covered in COWHIDE.

3 During the reign of Ramses II, from 1279 to 1213 B.C., soldiers sported helmets and LEATHER ARMOR covered with small SCALES.

4 Ancient Egyptian WARSHIPS had high SIDEWALLS to protect the oarsmen from attack.

5 Some ancient Egyptian ships had a weapon called a ram ON THE FRONT. The sailors WOULD STEER the boat into an enemy ship, causing the ram to smash through it.

25 MILITARY FACTS ABOUT WEAPONS,

6 One of the earliest weapons was a CRUSHING DEVICE CALLED A MACE, which consisted of a club with a rock attached to one end.

7 The mace was a symbol of power. Artworks of the time often depicted rulers CRUSHING their enemies with the MACE.

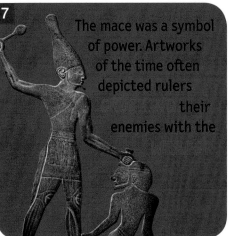

8 According to legend, ancient Egyptian SOLDIERS staged a SURPRISE ATTACK in Jaffa—an ancient city in present-day Israel—by HIDING IN SACKS OF GRAIN brought into the city.

9 Ancient Egypt's army was BROKEN UP INTO DIVISIONS of about 5,000 troops. Each division was NAMED AFTER A GOD.

10 The highest ranking military official, known as the OVERSEER OF THE ARMY, reported directly to the PHARAOH.

11 The ancient Egyptian military began using CHARIOTS around the 18th century B.C. Each chariot had two wheels and was pulled by TWO HORSES.

12 Each chariot held two soldiers—A DRIVER AND A FIGHTER who used a bow and arrow, sword, or javelin to attack the enemy.

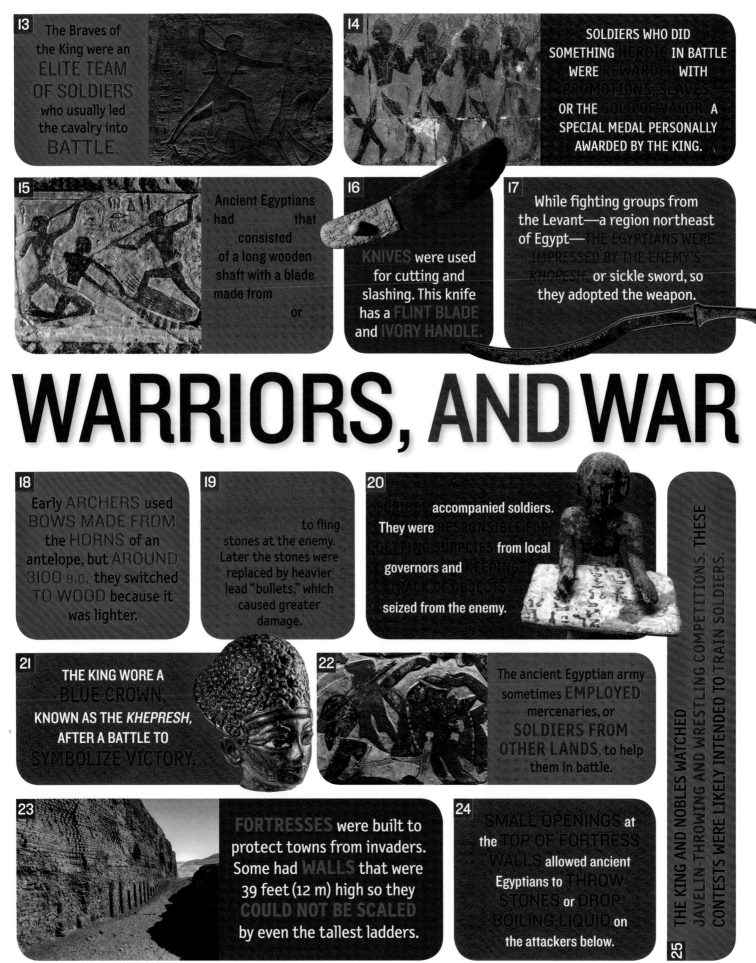

13 The Braves of the King were an ELITE TEAM OF SOLDIERS who usually led the cavalry into BATTLE.

14 SOLDIERS WHO DID SOMETHING HEROIC IN BATTLE WERE REWARDED WITH PROMOTIONS, SLAVES, OR THE GOLD OF VALOR, A SPECIAL MEDAL PERSONALLY AWARDED BY THE KING.

15 Ancient Egyptians had that consisted of a long wooden shaft with a blade made from or

16 KNIVES were used for cutting and slashing. This knife has a FLINT BLADE and IVORY HANDLE.

17 While fighting groups from the Levant—a region northeast of Egypt—THE EGYPTIANS WERE IMPRESSED BY THE ENEMY'S KHOPESH, or sickle sword, so they adopted the weapon.

WARRIORS, AND WAR

18 Early ARCHERS used BOWS MADE FROM the HORNS of an antelope, but AROUND 3100 B.C. they switched TO WOOD because it was lighter.

19 to fling stones at the enemy. Later the stones were replaced by heavier lead "bullets," which caused greater damage.

20 SCRIBES accompanied soldiers. They were RESPONSIBLE FOR GETTING SUPPLIES from local governors and KEEPING TRACK OF OBJECTS seized from the enemy.

21 THE KING WORE A BLUE CROWN, KNOWN AS THE *KHEPRESH*, AFTER A BATTLE TO SYMBOLIZE VICTORY.

22 The ancient Egyptian army sometimes EMPLOYED mercenaries, or SOLDIERS FROM OTHER LANDS, to help them in battle.

23 FORTRESSES were built to protect towns from invaders. Some had WALLS that were 39 feet (12 m) high so they COULD NOT BE SCALED by even the tallest ladders.

24 SMALL OPENINGS at the TOP OF FORTRESS WALLS allowed ancient Egyptians to THROW STONES or DROP BOILING LIQUID on the attackers below.

25 THE KING AND NOBLES WATCHED JAVELIN-THROWING AND WRESTLING COMPETITIONS. THESE CONTESTS WERE LIKELY INTENDED TO TRAIN SOLDIERS.

1 An ancient Egyptian sphinx was a mythical beast that often had a lion's body and a human's head. The head often depicted the reigning pharaoh.

2 Six granite sphinxes that depict the **female pharaoh Hatshepsut** have been discovered in her temple at Thebes.

3 The world's most famous sphinx—the Great Sphinx at Giza—was carved from a single piece of limestone and is the world's largest single-stone statue.

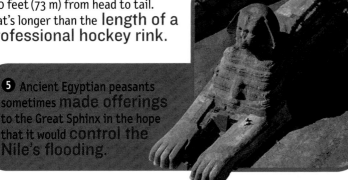

4 The Great Sphinx at Giza measures 240 feet (73 m) from head to tail. That's longer than the **length of a professional hockey rink.**

5 Ancient Egyptian peasants sometimes made offerings to the Great Sphinx in the hope that it would control the Nile's flooding.

6 Some historians believe the Great Sphinx's nose was broken by someone who **hated the peasants' devotion to the monument.**

7 Many experts believe that King Khafre who ruled Egypt sometime between 2520 and 2494 B.C., commissioned the sphinx because his pyramid is located nearby.

8 Traces of **blue, red,** and **yellow pigments** on the Great Sphinx suggest that the monument may originally have been brightly colored.

ABOUT SPHINXES

9 Two sphinxes that depict Amenhotep III were transported to St. Petersburg, Russia, in the 1830s. Both sphinxes wear the crowns of Upper and Lower Egypt.

10 During a dive off the northern coast of Egypt, a French archaeologist discovered a submerged **falcon-headed sphinx with the body of a crocodile.**

11 By the 1800s, the Great Sphinx had become a popular symbol of Egypt. It appeared on stamps and coins.

12 The **Great Sphinx once had a stone beard.** Fragments of the beard are on display at the British Museum in London, England.

13 Senwosret I, who ruled from 1918 to 1875 B.C., commissioned 150 statues—including 60 sphinxes of himself.

14 Some Egyptian sphinxes depict a **ram's head.** These sphinxes likely represent the **creator god Amun,** who could take the form of a ram.

15 Ancient Egyptians weren't the only people to create sphinxes. One ancient Roman sphinx depicts a lion's body, a woman's head, and an eagle's wings.

a modern guardian sphinx in Birmingham, England

1
Archaeologists discovered a tomb dedicated to Osiris, god of the underworld, in the ancient city of Thebes.

2
The "tomb of Osiris" contains a burial chamber for the god and a room with wall carvings that depict demons.

3
By studying human remains in Thebes, scientists have learned that a deadly plague spread through Egypt in the A.D. 200s.

4
According to scientists, plague victims likely had symptoms similar to those infected by the deadly Ebola virus.

5
Scans of an ancient Egyptian mummified bird show that it died eating a mouse.

6
Skeletons of six cats buried in an ancient Egyptian cemetery suggest that the Egyptians had pet cats at least 5,600 years ago.

7
Researchers have learned that Alexandria, Egypt, was built to align with the rising sun on July 20, 356 B.C., the birthday of the city's founder, Alexander the Great.

8
Archaeologists discovered seven pairs of shoes in an ancient temple in Luxor, Egypt. The shoes were 2,000 years old.

9
Scientists believe the world's first zoo was established in the ancient Egyptian capital of Hierakonpolis.

10
The remains of at least 112 animals have been discovered at the site of the Hierakonpolis zoo.

11
Rock-cut tombs more than 2,000 years old have been discovered in El-Kamin El-Sahrawi, in Upper Egypt.

12
Archaeologists discovered an alphabet that was carved into a limestone wall in Egypt's Western Desert about 4,000 years ago.

13
A portion of a 3,800-year-old pyramid was discovered in Dahshur, north of King Snefru's Bent Pyramid.

14
Scientists studying the remains of the Dahshur pyramid discovered a stone slab inscribed with the name of King Ameny Qemau, who ruled during the 13th dynasty.

15
The Dahshur pyramid was likely built for an earlier pharaoh, but King Ameny Qemau claimed it as his own.

16
A linen dress discovered in the town of Tarkhan, Egypt, is more than 5,000 years old.

17
The inscription on a coffin of an ancient Egyptian woman named Meresamun states that she was a "Singer in the Interior of the Temple of Amun in Karnak."

18
By studying Meresamun, scientists learned that she lived in Thebes in 800 B.C. and that her brightly colored coffin was made from cartonnage, similar to papier-mâché.

19
A bronze coffin made for a mummified cobra has been found in the shape of a snake with a human head.

20
A 3,500-year-old tomb belonging to a royal goldsmith was discovered near the Valley of the Kings. It contained mummies and statues of the goldsmith's family.

21
Also discovered near the valley was the tomb of an ancient Egyptian official named Userhat. The tomb contained 1,000 statues, wooden masks, and clay pots.

22
By analyzing bone samples from 151 mummies, scientists learned that ancient Egyptians were closely related to people from the Near East and southeastern Europe.

23
A 4,600-year-old funeral boat was unearthed from a site near Cairo, Egypt. The boat was intended to symbolically take the deceased pharaoh's spirit to the underworld.

24
Scientists discovered a chamber near the tomb of Senwosret III with images of boats on the walls. They believe the ruler's funeral boat was buried here.

25
The funeral boat of Senwosret III was buried 3,800 years ago but it was never found.

26
Archaeologists discovered a large temple devoted to the sun god, Ra, beneath a marketplace in Cairo, the modern capital of Egypt.

27
A pink granite statue weighing about 10,000 pounds (4,536 kg) was discovered in the excavated temple beneath Cairo.

28
After scanning the mummy of an Egyptian princess, scientists discovered a buildup of calcium in her body. This may have caused her heart and arteries to harden—causing a heart attack.

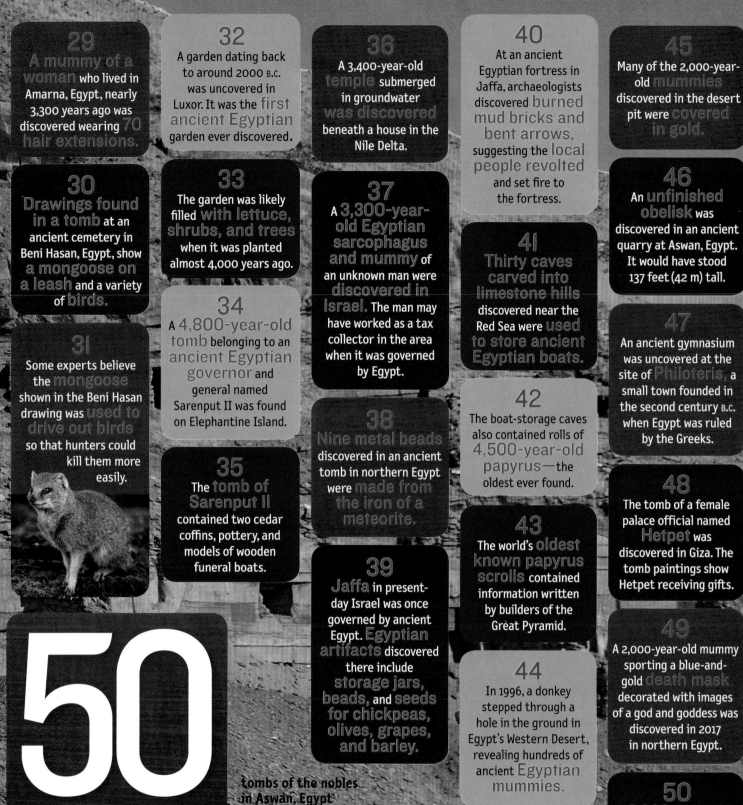

29
A mummy of a woman who lived in Amarna, Egypt, nearly 3,300 years ago was discovered wearing 70 hair extensions.

30
Drawings found in a tomb at an ancient cemetery in Beni Hasan, Egypt, show a mongoose on a leash and a variety of birds.

31
Some experts believe the mongoose shown in the Beni Hasan drawing was used to drive out birds so that hunters could kill them more easily.

32
A garden dating back to around 2000 B.C. was uncovered in Luxor. It was the first ancient Egyptian garden ever discovered.

33
The garden was likely filled with lettuce, shrubs, and trees when it was planted almost 4,000 years ago.

34
A 4,800-year-old tomb belonging to an ancient Egyptian governor and general named Sarenput II was found on Elephantine Island.

35
The tomb of Sarenput II contained two cedar coffins, pottery, and models of wooden funeral boats.

36
A 3,400-year-old temple submerged in groundwater was discovered beneath a house in the Nile Delta.

37
A 3,300-year-old Egyptian sarcophagus and mummy of an unknown man were discovered in Israel. The man may have worked as a tax collector in the area when it was governed by Egypt.

38
Nine metal beads discovered in an ancient tomb in northern Egypt were made from the iron of a meteorite.

39
Jaffa in present-day Israel was once governed by ancient Egypt. Egyptian artifacts discovered there include storage jars, beads, and seeds for chickpeas, olives, grapes, and barley.

40
At an ancient Egyptian fortress in Jaffa, archaeologists discovered burned mud bricks and bent arrows, suggesting the local people revolted and set fire to the fortress.

41
Thirty caves carved into limestone hills discovered near the Red Sea were used to store ancient Egyptian boats.

42
The boat-storage caves also contained rolls of 4,500-year-old papyrus—the oldest ever found.

43
The world's oldest known papyrus scrolls contained information written by builders of the Great Pyramid.

44
In 1996, a donkey stepped through a hole in the ground in Egypt's Western Desert, revealing hundreds of ancient Egyptian mummies.

45
Many of the 2,000-year-old mummies discovered in the desert pit were covered in gold.

46
An unfinished obelisk was discovered in an ancient quarry at Aswan, Egypt. It would have stood 137 feet (42 m) tall.

47
An ancient gymnasium was uncovered at the site of Philoteris, a small town founded in the second century B.C. when Egypt was ruled by the Greeks.

48
The tomb of a female palace official named Hetpet was discovered in Giza. The tomb paintings show Hetpet receiving gifts.

49
A 2,000-year-old mummy sporting a blue-and-gold death mask decorated with images of a god and goddess was discovered in 2017 in northern Egypt.

50
A 3,000-year-old Egyptian fortress was discovered in the ancient city of Tell El-Habua, near the Suez Canal. Soldiers there likely watched for approaching enemies from present-day Palestine.

tombs of the nobles in Aswan, Egypt

50
Unearthed Facts About
AMAZING FINDS

1 ONLY THE KING WAS ALLOWED TO MAKE LAWS IN ANCIENT EGYPT.

2 With the exception of slaves and servants, EVERYONE WAS CONSIDERED EQUAL before the law.

3 SERIOUS CRIMES such as murder were usually JUDGED BY THE VIZIER, and occasionally the PHARAOH.

4 The HIGHEST RANKING OFFICIAL in a royal estate JUDGED MINOR CRIMES, such as trading disputes, in a small outdoor court called a *kenbet*.

5 RELATIVES of a convicted criminal COULD BE IMPRISONED OR EXILED from Egypt.

25 VILLAINOUS FACTS ABOUT

6 Criminals AWAITING TRIAL were likely HELD IN a TEMPLE ROOM or a DEEP PIT.

7 TOMB ROBBING WAS CONSIDERED A TERRIBLE CRIME BECAUSE THE THIEF WAS NOT ONLY STEALING FROM THE DEAD BUT WAS ROBBING A PERSON IN THE AFTERLIFE.

8 Sometimes, tomb robbers received severe punishments such as **branding** or **100 strokes** with a cane.

9 In the village of Deir el-Medina, **CAPTURED THIEVES** were ordered to **RETURN STOLEN GOODS** and **PAY A FINE** of twice their value.

10 The GREAT PRISON IN THEBES was a large complex with HOLDING CELLS and COURTS, where criminals were tried. Records of court cases were also stored here.

11 In 2012, scientists studying the mummy of **RAMSES III** discovered the pharaoh **HAD BEEN MURDERED** with a deep gash to his throat.

12 Papyrus records documenting the death of Ramses III reveal that his wife, Queen Tiye, and son, Pentaweret, PLOTTED THE KING'S MURDER.

13 Archaeologists studying Pentaweret's mummified body noticed HIS MOUTH WAS OPEN IN A SCREAM. They believe the reaction was the result of Pentaweret's punishment—death by hanging.

14 Egypt's police force had many responsibilities. They protected farmers against theft, accompanied officials collecting taxes from the public, and patrolled borders.

15
Some police officers guarded public places with the HELP OF TRAINED DOGS OR MONKEYS SUCH AS BABOONS.

16 PRISONERS WHO TRIED TO ESCAPE sometimes had their EYES GOUGED AND NOSES CUT OFF before being returned to their captors.

17 People found guilty of committing SEVERE CRIMES could be EXECUTED. Some were even FED TO CROCODILES.

CRIME AND PUNISHMENT

18 The MEDJAY was a special POLICE FORCE that protected important places such as cemeteries.

19 Local residents could serve as GUARDIANS to WATCH OVER TOOLS used to build and decorate tombs.

20 The GREAT PYRAMID, commissioned by King Khufu, contained many passages and SECRET CHAMBERS to confuse criminals who were trying to find the ruler's treasures.

21 To punish one criminal for plotting to kill Ramses III, Egyptian authorities CHANGED THE CRIMINAL'S NAME to a title meaning "Ra[mses] hates him."

22 When a soldier deserted the army, his FAMILY was held HOSTAGE by Egyptian authorities until he returned. Then he was sentenced to HARD LABOR in a mine or quarry.

23 Anyone who RELEASED MILITARY SECRETS to ancient Egypt's enemies could have their TONGUE REMOVED.

24 A person ACCUSED of a crime HAD TO CONFESS TO WRONGDOING. If they refused to do so, they were sometimes thought innocent and released.

25 OFFICIALS SOMETIMES TRIED TO FORCE CONFESSIONS FROM SUSPECTS BY BEATING THEM.

1 Naukratis—located in the Nile Delta—was a Greek trading port for more than 1,000 years. It was eventually abandoned in the A.D. 600s.

2 Scientists have discovered Greek and Egyptian artifacts buried at the Naukratis site. These include Greek pottery, wood from Greek ships, and Egyptian statues.

3 During the A.D. 700s, earthquakes and floods caused areas of the Nile Delta—including the cities of Canopus and Thonis-Heracleion—to sink.

4 In 1933, Canopus was discovered by a British aircraft pilot who spotted underwater ruins as he flew over the Mediterranean Sea.

5 Parts of a temple to Isis, goddess of magic and the heavens, and a large granite statue believed to be either Cleopatra II or Cleopatra III were discovered at Thonis-Heracleion.

6 A large canal once linked the drowned cities of Thonis-Heracleion and Canopus. Archaeologists have discovered 69 ancient Egyptian boats in this region.

7 Underwater archaeologists discovered a pink granite statue of the Nile god Hapi while excavating Thonis-Heracleion. The statue was 16 feet (5 m) tall.

ABOUT LOST CITIES

8 Tanis, a city in the Nile Delta, was the capital of Egypt around 1075 B.C. Over time, the city was abandoned and covered by Nile silt.

9 In the 1930s, a French archaeologist excavated Tanis. He unearthed royal tombs filled with treasures such as jewelry, golden masks, and silver coffins.

10 In 2016, archaeologists announced that they had uncovered a portion of an ancient Egyptian city called Abydos that had been buried for 5,000 years. The ruins included several houses and a cemetery.

11 Archaeologists have also found evidence that as many as 16 unknown Egyptian rulers were buried in another newly discovered city of Abydos.

12 About 1,600 years ago, a series of earthquakes and a tsunami destroyed much of Alexandria, Egypt— a city founded by the Greeks in 331 B.C.

13 Divers excavating ruins near present-day Alexandria discovered giant statues that date back to Ramses II, who died in 1213 B.C.

14 In 2007, scientists analyzing sediment in Alexandria revealed that a 3,000-year-old unknown settlement once existed at the site—long before Alexandria was founded.

15 The ancient city of _____ was home to the _____ Experts believe stones from the Pharos were later used to build a nearby fort.

inside the sanctuary of the Temple of Seti, Abydos

1
Many factors contributed to the slow and steady fall of ancient Egypt, including political rivalries and economic problems.

2
Various groups attacked ancient Egypt. For example, around 1293 B.C., tribes from ancient Libya sparred with the Egyptians.

3
Libyan tribes joined forces with the Sea Peoples, a group from the Mediterranean region who wanted to settle in the Nile Delta—and invaded Egypt.

4
The Egyptians fended off the invading Libyan tribes and Sea Peoples when they first attacked in 1207 B.C. However, it was the first of many battles among the groups.

5
Although Egypt was victorious, the battles destroyed many Egyptian states along the Mediterranean Sea.

6
With the Egyptian states along the Mediterranean destroyed by invaders, ancient Egypt's economy suffered a blow.

7
Natural disasters also took a toll on the Egyptians. Sometimes, Nile flooding resulted in poor harvests.

8
When the harvests were poor, the price of grain could skyrocket to eight times the standard price.

9
In 1153 B.C. the vizier could supply only half the food needed to feed the tomb workers at Deir el-Medina, so the workers rioted.

10
Afterward, a wave of political corruption spread and King Ramses III was assassinated.

11
As a result of corruption and economic hardship in ancient Egypt, the king's power decreased throughout the 20th dynasty (1190 to 1069 B.C.).

Red Pyramid, Dashur, Egypt

12
During ancient Egypt's 20th dynasty, people asked statues of gods instead of the king to make important decisions.

13
The temple statues answered the Egyptians' questions with symbolic movements that were likely triggered by the priests who looked after them.

14
A high priest named Amenhotep had himself depicted as important as the king on a wall in Karnak.

15
After Amenhotep, a general named Herihor was named high priest and vizier. He became the most powerful official in Egypt.

16
When King Ramses XI died, the high priest took control of southern Egypt and an official named Nesbanebdjedet became king of northern Egypt.

17
Non-Egyptian pharaohs began to take over Egypt. Around 945 B.C. Egypt's King Psusennes II died without an heir, so his son-in-law Sheshonq I, an army general with Libyan roots—took over.

18
As pharaoh, Sheshonq I tried to unify Egypt by placing his family members in high positions. He even made his son high priest to regain control of Thebes.

19
During the ninth century B.C. the Nubian kingdom of Kush thrived. It built lavish structures the Nubians believed were superior to those of Egypt at the time.

20
Around 750 B.C. a Kushite king named Kashta marched into Upper Egypt with an army and declared himself king of Upper and Lower Egypt.

50 Fade-Away **Facts About** THE FALL OF ANCIENT EGYPT

21 About 80 years later, the Assyrians—a group from the east—invaded Egypt and eventually succeeded in driving out the Nubian king Taharqo.

22 To maintain control in Egypt, the Assyrians appointed Egyptians who were loyal to them to high-ranking positions.

23 Psamtik I was the son of an Assyrian loyalist who benefited from the association by being appointed king in 664 B.C.

24 Foreign rule continued in 525 B.C. when the Persians conquered Egypt and appointed an official to watch over the kingdom as they governed it from afar.

25 After their takeover of Egypt, the Persian regime plundered Egypt's temples.

26 Almost 200 years after the Persian takeover of ancient Egypt, Alexander the Great, a ruler from the kingdom of Macedon in northern Greece, freed Egypt.

27 Alexander's takeover of Egypt was met with little resistance as his troops outnumbered the Persian forces stationed in Egypt.

28 Ancient Egyptians thanked Alexander for liberating them from the Persians and crowned him king of the city of Memphis.

29 When Alexander died in 323 B.C. his body was buried in Alexandria, a city he founded in northern Egypt.

30 A Macedonian-Greek general, Ptolemy I, became Egypt's ruler in 304 B.C. He merged his culture with Egypt's.

31 After Ptolemy I's death, Egypt was ruled by a mixture of Egyptian and Macedonian-Greek leaders.

32 Fighting and scandal among top officials included Ptolemy XI having his wife, Berenice III, murdered after taking the throne.

33 The murder of Berenice III, a beloved queen, enraged the Egyptians. They dragged her assailant, King Ptolemy XI, from his palace and executed him.

34 In about 193 B.C. Ptolemy V married Cleopatra I, the daughter of a Syrian emperor. The marriage gave Egypt part of neighboring Syria.

35 Several years after the death of Cleopatra I, the Egyptians attacked Syria, believing it was theirs, but were defeated.

36 Syrian troops, led by Antiochus, counterattacked Egypt and moved in to conquer the kingdom.

37 The family of Antiochus had a history of sparring with Rome, so the Romans came to Egypt's rescue in 168 B.C. and ordered Antiochus to leave.

38 Rome continued to help Egypt for the next 130 years. This relationship would eventually lead to Egypt's demise.

39 Some rulers took desperate measures to remain in power. Ptolemy VIII, who ruled Egypt from 170 to 116 B.C., had his son murdered because he was a rival.

40 Ptolemy VIII also encouraged Roman interference. He promised Egypt to Rome if he died without an heir.

41 In about 48 B.C. Ptolemy XIII challenged his sister, Cleopatra, for the throne and had most of Egypt's support, but she won with the help of Roman general Julius Caesar.

42 In 47 B.C. Cleopatra VII was officially restored to the throne, which she now shared with her 11-year-old brother, Ptolemy XIV.

43 Caesar and Cleopatra developed a personal relationship and had a son together. As a result, Caesar was seen as a protector of Egypt.

44 By 44 B.C. Julius Caesar had become dictator of the Roman Empire and wished to marry Cleopatra, but he was assassinated by political rivals that same year.

45 Ptolemy XIV was murdered in 44 B.C.—likely at Cleopatra's command.

46 To maintain Rome's support, Cleopatra befriended a Roman general, Mark Antony, and eventually they made plans to rule Rome's eastern provinces.

47 Julius Caesar's great-nephew, Octavian, challenged Mark Antony and, in 31 B.C., a war erupted. Egypt sided with Antony.

48 Mark Antony's forces lost the battle, leaving Cleopatra vulnerable in Egypt.

49 In 30 B.C., Roman forces marched into Alexandria and conquered Egypt.

50 Cleopatra took her own life and, as much of Egypt became part of the Roman Empire, almost 3,000 years of Egyptian rule came to an end.

15 ENGAGING FACTS

1 Since 490 B.C. people have been traveling to Egypt to study its history and culture. This study is called Egyptology.

2 Early explorers of ancient Egypt used **dynamite** to get inside **rock-cut tombs** and likely destroyed artifacts in the process.

3 Today, scientists use radar technology to search for hidden tombs and chambers before determining the best way to access the rooms without damaging them.

4 **3D printing,** a technology that uses various materials to print three-dimensional objects, has been **used to re-create ancient Egyptian artifacts.** This helps archaeologists study new findings without damaging the real thing.

5 To create a detailed map of the Great Pyramid, archaeologist Yukinori Kawae has used drones—small, pilotless aircraft—to take digital photos of the structure from angles that are difficult for humans to reach.

6 Kawae has also used heat-detecting **thermal cameras to identify heat coming from stones at the bottom of the pyramid.** This suggests a secret chamber may be hidden beneath the base.

7 Early Egyptologists studied mummies by **unwrapping their bandages** and **dissecting the bodies.**

8 In 1895 a German scientist became the first person to take **x-rays of a mummy.** This allowed him to study the body without destroying its bandages.

9 Many experts study mummies with CT scans, which provide them with a detailed view of the body and help them to identify health issues.

10 **Endoscopes**—long, thin tubes with a small camera at one end—are sometimes inserted into mummies to **look at their organs and bones.**

11 Egyptologists sometimes use **robots to access hard-to-reach places.** In 2014 a robot explored the tunnels of the Great Pyramid.

12 Sarah Parcak is a "**space archaeologist**" who **uses satellites to locate lost ancient Egyptian sites.**

13 In 2010 Parcak used satellite technology to locate the lost pyramid of Amenemhet III, a pharaoh who ruled from 1818 to 1770 B.C.

14 British archaeologist **Sir Flinders Petrie** is considered the "father of archaeology" for his many finds—including 3,000 graves of early settlers in **ancient Egypt.**

15 Egyptologists have discovered that mummies still contain DNA—molecules with their genetic information. By extracting this DNA in a laboratory, researchers can study how Egyptians have changed over time.

the recently discovered tomb of the goldsmith Amenemhat

GLOSSARY

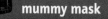

mummy mask

afterlife a world or existence that some people believe they enter after death

amulet a charm worn for its magical or protective powers

archaeologist a person who studies human history based on objects from the past

archaeology the study of human history based on remains dug up or uncovered

bacteria tiny, single-celled organisms

bust a sculpture or other artwork representing a person's head and shoulders

canal a waterway made by humans, often to irrigate, or supply water to, farmland

canopic jar one of four containers used by ancient Egyptians to hold the stomach, intestines, lungs, and liver removed from a body during the mummification process

capital a city where a region's or country's government is located

cartouche an oval border around an ancient Egyptian ruler's name

cataract a rush of water around large rocks that obstruct a river's flow

ceremony an activity to celebrate or honor an event

chamber a room or section that has been sealed off from other sections

death mask of Tutankhamun

chantress a woman in ancient Egypt whose role was to sing or chant in a temple

chariot a vehicle with two or four wheels that is pulled by horses

class a division in society based on salary earned and type of job

coffin a box built to contain the body of a dead person

commemorate to honor an event or person

constellation a group of stars that form a recognizable shape in the night sky

coronation the ceremony or act of officially crowning a ruler

CT scan short for computerized tomography; a medical examination in which sections of a body are shown on a computer screen

curse a spell that is cast to cause harm or misfortune

dam a structure built across a river or other waterway to help control the flow of water

decipher to figure out or interpret

delta a flat, low-lying area that forms at the mouth of a river from deposits of sediments

Demotic a very cursive-style written language of ancient Egypt from 700 B.C. to A.D. 400

descendants children, grandchildren, and other offspring

DNA a chemical code that contains information about a living thing's body, such as eye and hair color; DNA stands for deoxyribonucleic acid

dynasty a sequence of rulers related by family or marriage

Egyptologist a person who studies ancient Egyptian culture and history

embalm to treat a dead body in a way that protects it from decay

embroider to decorate with elaborate sewing or needlework

endoscope a long, thin tube with a camera at one end designed to look inside the body

entomb to place in a tomb

excavate to expose or uncover by digging up sand, dirt, or rubble

expedition a journey with a specific purpose, such as exploration

fertile referring to soil, one that is rich in minerals, ideal for growing crops

fresco art or design painted directly onto the wet plaster of a wall or other surface

funerary having to do with ceremonies surrounding a funeral or burial

galena a lead-based mineral used in ancient Egyptian makeup

god a male spiritual or supreme being; ancient Egyptians had many gods

goddess a female spiritual or supreme being; ancient Egyptians had many goddesses

henna a plant that produces a reddish brown dye

hieroglyphs an ancient script made up of pictures that represent sounds, words, or concepts

inscribe to mark or engrave a surface

kingdom a government with a king or queen as its leader, or a land ruled by a king or queen

kohl a black powder, made of crushed minerals and other materials, used as eye makeup

linen a light, thin fabric made from the fibers of a flax plant

Maat a concept meaning truth, order, and justice in the universe

mace a weapon consisting of a club with a heavy object at one end

mastaba an ancient Egyptian tomb with sloping sides and a flat roof

mineral a natural substance that is formed underground, such as diamond or salt

stela showing three gods

mummification the process of preserving the corpse of a person or animal, either naturally, by environmental conditions, or through human techniques

mummy the corpse of a person or animal that has been preserved by the environment or by human techniques

natron a type of salt used to dry up dead bodies during the mummification process

necropolis a cemetery or burial ground

nemes a striped headcloth worn by Egyptian rulers

nilometer a structure that was used for measuring the water level of the Nile, especially during flooding

nomarch an official who governed a nome, or province, in ancient Egypt

nome a province of ancient Egypt

oasis an area made suitable for growing crops by a source of freshwater in an otherwise dry region

obelisk a tall, four-sided stone structure that tapers to a pyramid shape on top

organ a group of tissues in the body that perform a specific task

ostraca pieces of pottery or stone that were written on

papyrus a reed plant that can be sliced and pounded into a piece of paperlike writing material, also called papyrus

parasite an organism that lives and feeds on or in other living things

pharaoh a king of ancient Egypt; the word originally meant "great house"

plague a wide-spreading disease, or a large gathering of a species, harmful to living things

preserve to maintain and keep safe from damage

priest title of a religious leader in many faiths

purify to cleanse thoroughly

pyramid a structure with a square base and triangular sides that meet in a point

model mummy case

relief a type of sculpture in which shapes or figures are raised above or sunken beneath the surrounding surface

resin a clear, sticky substance made by some plants

sakia a large rotating wheel used to collect water

sarcophagus a stone coffin, usually decorated with scenes and texts

scarab a dung beetle sacred to ancient Egyptians

scribe a person who works as a professional writer or record keeper

sediment solid material moved and deposited by water, ice, or wind

senet an Egyptian board game

shabti a figure, often resembling a mummified image of the deceased, that was buried with a person for the purpose of working on behalf of the deceased in the afterlife

shaduf a pole with a bucket on one end and a counterweight on the other end used for collecting and lifting water from the Nile

side lock a hairstyle worn by children in ancient Egypt, consisting of a long lock of hair growing from the side of an otherwise shaved scalp

sistrum a handheld musical instrument that rattles when shaken

sphinx an image of a resting lion with the head of a human, ram, or hawk

statue of a cat

spirit the apparent life force of a person that includes their character and feelings

stela a stone or wood slab with carvings

temple a building used for worship

throne a chair used by a king or queen at special ceremonies or events

tomb an enclosed burial place

underworld in mythology, a place for spirits of the dead

vizier a high-ranking official who reported directly to the ruler of ancient Egypt

TOMB OF SETI I

statuette
of Seti I

A Royal Tomb

King Seti I, who ruled Egypt from 1290 to 1279 B.C. was buried inside a large tomb carved into the limestone cliffs of the Valley of the Kings. Take a look inside Seti's tomb and discover how it was built and used. The king's sarcophagus would have been brought in from the entrance to the right and placed in the burial chamber.

sculptors chiseling reliefs into the tomb wall

unfinished chamber

stonecutter chiseling out a chamber

plasterer preparing a rough wall for art by smoothing the surface

burial chamber of the king

stonecutter hauling stones

limestone cliff

corridor leading to the entrance/exit

scaffolding

stone sarcophagus that would hold the king's mummy after death

artist drawing an outline on the wall

master painter adding details to the art on the tomb wall

stone pillar used to support the roof of the tomb

TIMELINE

stone
sphinx

Timeline of Ancient Egyptian Civilization

The ancient Egyptian civilization spanned thousands of years. Take a look at some of the key moments.

6000 B.C.

Early settlers arrive in the Nile Valley, where they fish and hunt. They also make pottery and tools from bone and stone.

5200 B.C.

The Nile settlers start to farm crops, such as barley and wheat, and raise animals such as sheep, goats, and pigs.

4500 B.C.

Simple houses and buildings are made from mud bricks, and stone is used to make small statues and figures.

4000 B.C.

The settlers start to use technology when they produce jewelry by covering a whitish stone called steatite in a clear blue glaze.

3250 B.C.

Early Egyptians begin to use a writing system with hieroglyphs—symbols that stand for words and sounds— to document information.

3200 B.C.

Traveling up and down the Nile River becomes easier thanks to sails hoisted on boats.

3100 B.C.*

King Narmer unites the separate communities living around the Nile as one kingdom.

3000 B.C.

Papyrus stems are sliced and pressed together to make the first paperlike writing material.

2530 B.C.

The Great Pyramid at Giza is built as a tomb for King Khufu.

2520–2494 B.C.

The Great Sphinx—a large monument with the body of a lion and the head of a human—is created, likely for King Khafre.

*This is an estimate based on historical data. You may see different dates for this event.

2180–2160 B.C.

Food supplies run low when the Nile fails to provide enough water—and nutrients—to nourish the land during its annual floods. Many Egyptians starve.

2080–1938 B.C.

Construction of the Karnak Temple begins—likely when the ruler Intef II has a sandstone column built at the site.

2000–1500 B.C.

Ancient Egyptians expand trade with neighboring countries and regions such as Nubia, Syria, and Palestine.

1481–1099 B.C.

After pyramid tombs are raided by robbers, Egyptian rulers make arrangements to be buried in hidden tombs in an isolated valley in the ancient city of Thebes. Today, this valley is known as the Valley of the Kings.

1353 B.C.

Akhenaten becomes king and creates a revolution in Egypt when he declares Aten, a sun god, the one and only god.

1332 B.C.

The young king Tutankhamun takes the throne. His rule lasts only 10 years, but the discovery of his nearly complete tomb in A.D. 1922 makes him a legend.

1075 B.C.

Egypt is divided into two lands—Upper Egypt ruled by the high priest, and Lower Egypt ruled by the king.

750–332 B.C.

For more than 400 years, Egypt is conquered and ruled by various groups, including the Nubians, Assyrians, and Persians.

332 B.C.

Alexander the Great—a Macedonian leader from northern Greece—frees Egypt from its Persian rulers. Eventually, the city of Alexandria is established in his honor.

30 B.C.

Ancient Egypt's final ruler, Cleopatra VII, dies and Egypt falls to the ancient Romans.

Ancient Egypt's Dynasties and Rulers

To historians, "ancient Egypt" lasted for almost 3,000 years. They divide this time into sections called periods. Some periods were prosperous for ancient Egyptians. They were marked by a strong economy and wartime victories. Other periods—known as "intermediate periods"—were disastrous, and riddled with attacks, disease, and famine. Each period had its own dynasty—a sequence of rulers that were related.

Dates and Names

The dates given below are estimates based on historical data, which in some periods are poor or missing. This is why some periods overlap. The names of rulers have been translated from an ancient language and vary among scholars, so you may find different spellings in other reference books.

EARLY DYNASTIC PERIOD, 2950–2575 B.C.

First Dynasty, 2950–2750 B.C.
Narmer
Aha
Djer
Neith-Hotep
Djet
Merneith
Den
Anedjib
Semerkhet
Qaa

Second Dynasty, 2750–2650 B.C.
Hetepsekhemwy
Nebra
Ninetjer
Peribsen
Khasekhem

Third Dynasty, 2650–2575 B.C.
Djoser
Sekhemkhet
Khaba
Sanakht
Huni

OLD KINGDOM, 2575–2125 B.C.

Fourth Dynasty, 2575–2450 B.C.
Snefru, 2575–2545
Khufu, 2545–2525
Djedefra, 2525–2520
Khafre, 2520–2494
Menkaure
Shepseskaf

Fifth Dynasty, 2450–2325 B.C.
Userkaf
Sahura
Neferirkara Kakai
Shepseskara Izi
Neferefra
Niuserra Ini
Menkauhor
Djedkara Isesi
Unas, 2350–2325

Sixth Dynasty, 2325–2175 B.C.
Teti
Userkara
Pepi I, 2315–2275
Merenra
Nitocris
Pepi II, 2260–2175

Seventh Dynasty
No details are known.

Eighth Dynasty, 2175–2125 B.C.
Eighteen kings, including the following:
Nemtyemsaf II
Neitiqerty Siptah
Ibi
Neferkaura
Neferkauhor
Neferirkara

FIRST INTERMEDIATE PERIOD, 2125–2010 B.C.

Ninth/Tenth Dynasty, 2125–1975 B.C.
Several kings, including the following:
Kheti I
Kheti II
Merikara

Eleventh Dynasty, 2080–1938 B.C.
Intef I
Intef II
Intef III

MIDDLE KINGDOM, 2010–1630 B.C.

Mentuhotep II, 2010–1960
Mentuhotep III, 1960–1948
Mentuhotep IV, 1948–1938

Twelfth Dynasty, 1938–1755 B.C.
Amenemhet I, 1938–1908
Senwosret I, 1918–1875
Amenemhet II, 1876–1842
Senwosret II, 1842–1837
Senwosret III, 1836–1818
Amenemhet III, 1818–1770
Amenemhet IV, 1770–1760
Sobeknefru, 1760–1755

Thirteenth Dynasty, 1755–1630 B.C.
At least 50 kings, including the following:
Sobekhotep III
Ameny Qemau

SECOND INTERMEDIATE PERIOD, 1630–1539 B.C.

Fourteenth Dynasty
Several kings, beginning with
Nehesy

Fifteenth Dynasty, 1630–1520 B.C.
Six kings, including the following:
Khyan, 1610–1570
Apepi, 1570–1530
Khamudi, 1530–1520

Sixteenth Dynasty
Numerous kings, including the following:
Neferhotep III
Mentuhotepi

Seventeenth Dynasty, 1630–1539 B.C.
Numerous kings, including the following:
Rahotep
Nubkheperra Intef
Sobekemsaf II
Seqenenre Tao II, 1545–1541
Kamose, 1541–1539

NEW KINGDOM, 1539–1069 B.C.

Eighteenth Dynasty, 1539–1292 B.C.
Ahmose, 1539–1514
Amenhotep I, 1514–1493
Thutmose I, 1493–1481
Thutmose II, 1481–1479
Thutmose III, 1479–1425, and
   Hatshepsut, 1473–1458
Amenhotep II, 1426–1400
Thutmose IV, 1400–1390
Amenhotep III, 1390–1353

Akhenaten, 1353–1336
Neferneferuaten, 1336–1332
Smenkhkara, 1336–1332
Tutankhamun, 1332–1322
Ay, 1322–1319
Horemheb, 1319–1292

Nineteenth Dynasty, 1292–1190 B.C.
Ramses I, 1292–1290
Seti I, 1290–1279
Ramses II, 1279–1213
Merenptah, 1213–1204
Seti II, 1204–1198
Amenmesse, 1204–1200
Siptah, 1198–1193
Tawosret, 1198–1190

Twentieth Dynasty, 1190–1069 B.C.
Sethnakht, 1190–1187
Ramses III, 1187–1156
Ramses IV, 1156–1150
Ramses V, 1150–1145
Ramses VI, 1145–1137
Ramses VII, 1137–1129
Ramses VIII, 1129–1126
Ramses IX, 1126–1108
Ramses X, 1108–1099
Ramses XI, 1099–1069

THIRD INTERMEDIATE PERIOD, 1069–664 B.C.

Twenty-first Dynasty, 1069–945 B.C.
Nesbanebdjedet, 1069–1045
Herihor, 1069–1063
Pinedjem I, 1063–1033
Amenemnisu, 1045–1040
Psusennes I, 1040–985
Amenemope, 985–975
Pinedjem II, 985–960
Osorkon the Elder, 975–970
Siamun, 970–950
Psusennes II, 950–945

Twenty-second Dynasty, 945–715 B.C.
Sheshonq I, 945–925
Osorkon I, 925–890
Sheshonq II, 890
Takelot I, 890–874
Osorkon II, 874–835
Sheshonq III, 835–793
Sheshonq IV, 793–783
Pamay, 785–777
Sheshonq V, 777–740
Padibastet II, 740–730
Osorkon IV, 735–715

Twenty-third Dynasty, 838–720 B.C.
Takelot II, 838–812
Padibastet I, 827–802
Iuput I, 812–802
Sheshonq VI, 802–796
Osorkon III, 796–768
Takelot III, 773–754
Rudamun, 754–735
Iny, 735–730
Peftjauawybast, 730–720

Twenty-fourth Dynasty, 740–715 B.C.
Tefnakht, 740–720
Bakenrenef, 720–715

Twenty-fifth Dynasty, 728–657 B.C.
Piankhi, 747–716
Sabaqo, 716–702
Shabitqo, 702–690
Taharqo, 690–664
Tanutamun, 664–657

LATE PERIOD, 664–332 B.C.

Twenty-sixth Dynasty, 664–525 B.C.
Psamtek I, 664–610
Nekau II, 610–595
Psamtek II, 595–589
Wahibra, 589–570
Ahmose II, 570–526
Psamtek III, 526–525

Twenty-seventh Dynasty, 525–404 B.C.
Cambyses, 525–522
Darius I, 522–486
Xerxes I, 486–465
Artaxerxes I, 465–424
Darius II, 424–404

Twenty-eighth Dynasty, 404–399 B.C.
Amenidiris, 404–399

Twenty-ninth Dynasty, 399–380 B.C.
Nepherites I, 399–393
Hakoris, 393–392
Pashermut, 392–391
Hakoris (restored), 391–380
Nepherites II, 380

Thirtieth Dynasty, 380–343 B.C.
Nectanebo I, 380–362
Djedher, 365–360
Nectanebo II, 360–343

Thirty-first Dynasty, 343–332 B.C.
Artaxerxes III, 343–338
Arses, 338–336
Darius III, 335–332

MACEDONIAN DYNASTY, 332–309 B.C.

Alexander the Great, 332–323
Philip III, 323–317
Alexander IV, 317–309

PTOLEMAIC PERIOD, 309–30 B.C.

Ptolemy I, 304–282
Ptolemy II, 285–246
Ptolemy III, 246–221
Ptolemy IV, 221–204
Ptolemy V, 204–180
Ptolemy VI, 180–145
Ptolemy VIII and Cleopatra II, 170–116
Ptolemy IX, 116–107, and Cleopatra III, 116–101
Ptolemy X, 107–88
Ptolemy IX, 88–80
Ptolemy XI and Berenice III, 80
Ptolemy XII, 80–58
Cleopatra VI, 58–57, and Berenice IV, 58–55
Ptolemy XII (restored), 55–51
Cleopatra VII, 51–30
   and Ptolemy XIII, 51–47
   and Ptolemy XIV, 47–44
   and Ptolemy XV Caesarion, 44–30

INDEX

gold
statuette

RESOURCES

Websites

National Geographic Exploring Ancient Egyptian Mysteries
Get facts about ancient Egypt and meet an Egyptologist to check out an x-ray of King Tutankhamun's body.
natgeokids.com/uk/discover/history/egypt/tutankhamun-facts
natgeokids.com/explore/history/king-tut-ancient-egyptian-mysteries

Fast Facts: Egypt
Travel to present-day Egypt to learn about the country's people, wildlife, and geography.
scholastic.com/teachers/articles/teaching-content/fast-facts-egypt

BBC Building the Great Pyramid
Discover how ancient Egyptian workers built the Great Pyramid at Giza.
bbc.co.uk/history/ancient/egyptians/great_pyramid_01.shtml

PBS Egypt's Golden Empire
Explore Egyptian society, religion, art, and so much more.
pbs.org/empires/egypt

Videos

Life After Death in Ancient Egypt
Unlock the secrets of a 4,400-year-old tomb.
nationalgeographic.org/video/life-after-death-in-ancient-egypt

History Channel: Ancient Egypt
Watch short videos about the Great Sphinx, ancient Egyptian medicine, and more.
history.com/topics/ancient-history/ancient-egypt/videos

Egypt's Lost Rival
Discover a city that challenged the ancient Egyptian empire. National Geographic Channel, 2011.

Treasures of Ancient Egypt
Uncover some of ancient Egypt's artistic treasures. BBC, 2014.

Books

Everything Ancient Egypt
By Crispin Boyer. National Geographic Kids, 2012.
Discover fascinating facts about pyramids, mummies, and more.

Inside Out: Egyptian Mummy
By Lorraine Jean Hopping. becker&mayer! kids, 2017.
"Unwrap" a model of an Egyptian mummy—and read about tombs, hieroglyphs, and the afterlife while you're at it.

The Treasury of Egyptian Mythology
By Donna Jo Napoli. National Geographic Kids, 2013.
Read spellbinding tales about Egyptian gods, goddesses, and legendary beasts.

You Wouldn't Want to Be Cleopatra!
By Jim Pipe. Franklin Watts, 2017.
Read a humorous account about the rise and fall of ancient Egypt's final ruler.

Places to Visit

British Museum, London, England
Egyptian Museum, Berlin, Germany
Egyptian Museum, Cairo, Egypt
Louvre Museum, Paris, France
Metropolitan Museum of Art, New York City, United States
Museum of Fine Arts, Boston, MA, United States
Penn Museum, Philadelphia, PA, United States
Smithsonian National Museum of Natural History, Washington, D.C., United States

CREDITS

PRODUCED FOR NATIONAL GEOGRAPHIC PARTNERS BY BENDER RICHARDSON WHITE

Since 1888, the National Geographic Society has funded more than 12,000 research, exploration, and preservation projects around the world. The Society receives funds from National Geographic Partners, LLC, funded in part by your purchase. A portion of the proceeds from this book supports this vital work. To learn more, visit natgeo.com/info.

NATIONAL GEOGRAPHIC and Yellow Border Design are trademarks of the National Geographic Society, used under license.

For more information, visit nationalgeographic.com, call 1-800-647-5463, or write to the following address:

National Geographic Partners
1145 17th Street N.W.
Washington, D.C. 20036-4688 U.S.A.

Visit us online at nationalgeographic.com/books

For librarians and teachers: ngchildrensbooks.org

More for kids from National Geographic: natgeokids.com

National Geographic Kids magazine inspires children to explore their world with fun yet educational articles on animals, science, nature, and more. Using fresh storytelling and amazing photography, *Nat Geo Kids* shows kids ages 6 to 14 the fascinating truth about the world—and why they should care.
kids.nationalgeographic.com/subscribe

For information about special discounts for bulk purchases, please contact National Geographic Books Special Sales: specialsales@natgeo.com

For rights or permissions inquiries, please contact National Geographic Books Subsidiary Rights: bookrights@natgeo.com

Cover designed by Brett Challos

Library of Congress Cataloging-in-Publication Data

Names: Honovich, Nancy, author.
Title: 1,000 facts about ancient Egypt / by Nancy Honovich.
Description: Washington, DC : National Geographic Kids, 2019. | Includes index.
Identifiers: LCCN 2018031312| ISBN 9781426332739 (hardcover) | ISBN 9781426332746 (hardcover)
Subjects: LCSH: Egypt--History--Juvenile literature. | Egypt--Geography--Juvenile literature.
Classification: LCC DT49 .H66 2019 | DDC 932--dc23
LC record available at https://lccn.loc.gov/2018031312

The publisher would like to thank Dr. Jennifer Houser Wegner, University of Pennsylvania, for careful review of this book, and the production team of Bender Richardson White: Lionel Bender, editor/project manager; Nancy Honovich, author; Catherine Farley, copy editor/proofreader; Ben White, art director; Sharon Dortenzio, picture editor; Malcolm Smythe, designer; Kim Richardson, production manager; Amanda Rock, fact-checker; Amron Gravett, indexer.

Printed in China
18/RRDS/1